Sing the Faith

D0067795

Pew Edition

Geneva Press
Louisville, Kentucky

INTRODUCTION

In the summer of 2002, the Presbyterian Publishing Corporation asked the General Assembly Council's Office of Research Services to conduct a survey related to the use of music in congregations. In one section, the survey specifically asked pastors and church musicians to comment on their desire for a supplement to the *Presbyterian Hymnal*, which was published in 1990. Based on the participants' enthusiastic response, PPC began working with church musicians and representatives of local congregations to shape a collection that would fit the needs of our denomination. *Sing the Faith* is the result of that effort.

This supplement to the *Presbyterian Hymnal* presents some of the best offerings in new congregational music from around the world, as well as old favorites and historic classics that the latest denominational hymnal does not contain. As a whole, the collection is designed to complement the hymnal and to give music leaders more choices of songs. In addition to the old favorites and historic classics, musical styles include newer hymns written in a traditional style; music from Europe, Africa, and Asia; African American and Hispanic American music; liturgical chants from the Taizé community; and more contemporary contributions.

Sing the Faith also includes variations on a few hymns that are in the *Presbyterian Hymnal*. In these cases, the hymns have new musical settings, significant word changes, or both.

This volume is the Pew edition, designed for congregational use. Harmony is provided where the congregation is to sing in parts. Where the congregation is to sing in unison, only the melody line is provided. (For more voice and instrumental variations, including guitar chords, see the Accompanist edition.)

Ages ago, the psalmist invited people of faith to lift their voices together in songs of thanks and praise, affirming that as one way to encounter God (Ps. 30:4). As part of today's faith community, we stand within the same invitation and promise. Thus, *Sing the Faith* is offered to Presbyterian congregations as an aid to the experience of and response to God in worship.

Davis Perkins, President and Publisher
Geneva Press
Presbyterian Publishing Corporation

SING THE FAITH
Pew Edition

Adaptation and new compilation
Copyright © 2003 by Geneva Press
Adapted and compiled by permission from
The Faith We Sing Copyright © 2000 Abingdon Press

This book is printed on acid-free paper.

ISBN-13: 978-0-664-50240-9
ISBN-10: 0-664-50240-7

09 10 11 12 — 10

MANUFACTURED IN THE UNITED STATES OF AMERICA

We Sing to You, O God

2001

1. We sing to you, O God, the Rock who gave us birth, let our re-joic-ing sing your name in all the earth. To you, O God, let songs be raised, in joy-ful hymns, our feast of praise.

2. We wan-dered far from home out in a des-ert land, you shield-ed with your love our fear-ful pil-grim band. You kept us safe with-in your arms and shel-tered us a-gainst the storm.

3. You bear us through the world, an ea-gle to her young, who ris-es on her wings and bears us toward the sun. We ride the vaults of light and air and trust in your un-fail-ing care.

4. O God, e-ter-nal God, we hide with-in your wings, the ev-er-last-ing arms to whom our prais-es ring. Your word is true, your way is just, you are the God in whom we trust.

WORDS: Gracia Grindal (Deut. 32:11, 18; 33:27; Ps. 57:1; 66:2; 96:1-2)
MUSIC: John Darwall; harm. from *Hymns Ancient and Modern*, 1875, alt.

Words © 1993 Selah Publishing Co., Inc.

DARWALL'S 148th
66.66.88

2002   I Will Call upon the Lord

Part 1 (melody)

I will call up-on the Lord

Part 2 (echo)

I will call up-on the

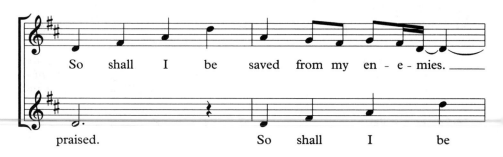

who is wor-thy to be praised.

Lord   who is wor-thy to be

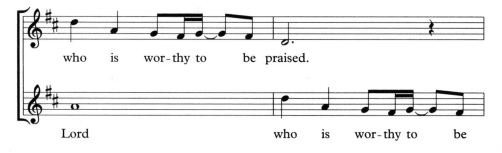

So shall I be saved from my en - e - mies. _____

praised.   So shall I be

— I will call up-on the Lord.

saved from my en - e - mies.   I will call up-on the Lord.

WORDS: Michael O'Shields (Ps. 18:1-2)
MUSIC: Michael O'Shields

I WILL CALL
Irregular with Refrain

Refrain

The Lord liv-eth, and bless-ed be the Rock; and let the God _

_ of my sal-va-tion be ex-alt-ed. The

Lord liv-eth, and bless-ed be the Rock; and let the God _

_ of my sal-va-tion be ex-alt-ed.

Praise You 2003

Praise you, praise you; let my life praise you. Praise

you, praise you; let my life, O Lord, praise you. Praise

you. Let my life, O Lord, praise you.

Stanzas included in other editions.

WORDS: Elizabeth Goodine
MUSIC: Elizabeth Goodine

PRAISE YOU
Irregular

2004 Praise the Source of Faith and Learning

1. Praise the source of faith and learn - ing that has
2. God of wis - dom, we ac - knowl-edge that our
3. May our faith re - deem the blun - der of be -
4. As two cur - rents in a riv - er fight each

sparked and stoked the mind with a pas - sion
sci - ence and our art and the breadth of
liev - ing that our thought has dis - placed the
oth - er's un - der - tow till con - verg - ing

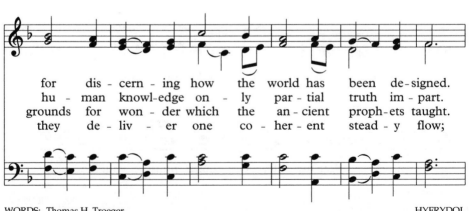

for dis - cern - ing how the world has been de-signed.
hu - man knowl-edge on - ly par - tial truth im - part.
grounds for won - der which the an - cient proph-ets taught.
they de - liv - er one co - her - ent stead - y flow;

WORDS: Thomas H. Troeger
MUSIC: Rowland H. Prichard; harm. from *The English Hymnal*

HYFRYDOL
87.87 D

Let the sense of won - der flow - ing from the
Far be - yond our cal - cu - la - tion lies a
May our learn - ing curb the er - ror which un -
blend, O God, our faith and learn - ing till they

won - ders we sur - vey keep our faith for -
depth we can - not sound where your pur - pose
think - ing faith can breed lest we jus - ti -
carve a sin - gle course, till they join as

ev - er grow - ing and re - new our need to pray:
for cre - a - tion and the pulse of life are found.
fy some ter - ror with an an - ti - quat - ed creed.
one, re - turn - ing praise and thanks to you, their Source.

2005   Arise, Shine

A-rise, shine; for your light has come,

A-rise, shine; for your

and the glo-ry of the Lord

light has come, and the

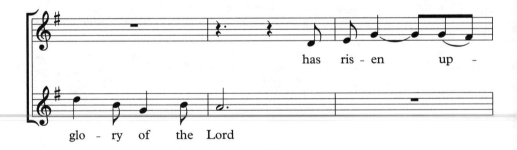

has ris-en up -

glo-ry of the Lord

on you.

has ris-en up - on you.

WORDS: Gary Alan Smith (Isa. 60:1)
MUSIC: Gary Alan Smith

ARISE, SHINE
Irregular

Lord God, Almighty

2006

1., 2. Lord God, Al - might - y, Sav - ior, Re - deem - er,
3. Fa - ther, we praise you. Je - sus, we love you.

on - ly true God to be wor - shiped and praised:
Spir - it, we thank you for the gifts of new life:

How can we tell you how much we love you?

Take now our lives, Lord, and teach us to love.

Stanzas included in other editions.

WORDS: Coni Huisman
MUSIC: Coni Huisman

COMFORT
Irregular

© 1984 Coni Huisman

Holy, Holy, Holy

(Santo, Santo, Santo)

2007

Ho - ly, ho - ly, ho - ly. My heart, my heart a - dores you! My
¡San - to, san - to, san - to, mi co - ra - zón te a - do - ra! Mi

heart knows how to say to you: You are ho - ly, Lord!
co - ra - zón te sa - be de - cir: ¡San - to e - res, Dios!

WORDS: Argentine folk song (Isa. 6:3)
MUSIC: Argentine folk song

SANTO
Irregular

2008   Ours Is a Singing Faith!

1. Ours is a sing-ing faith! Now hear the hymns we raise, re-
2. Ours is a sing-ing faith! Through all the ebb and flow of
3. Ours is a sing-ing faith! Up - held by work and prayer that
4. Ours is a sing-ing faith! All thanks to God be sung by

sound-ing, strong, the years a - long, and ech - o - ing our praise.
youth and age, on his-tory's page we see saints come and go.
jus - tice, peace, and hope not cease but flour-ish ev - ery - where.
peo - ple here both far and near in ev - ery land and tongue.

Ours is a sing-ing faith! In con - fi-dence we sing: cre -
Ours is a sing-ing faith! The mel - o - dy rolls on, sus -
Ours is a sing-ing faith! Though grief or pain hold sway, Christ
Ours is a sing-ing faith! Let psalms and an - thems rise from

a - tion's throne is God's a - lone, so joy - ous voic - es ring.
tained by those whose voic-es rose in praise in times long gone.
still shall dwell, Em - man-u - el! God with us all the way.
sun and moon and stars in tune till mu - sic fills the skies!

WORDS: Jane Parker Huber   SANDSTONE
MUSIC: Arthur Frackenpohl   SMD

O God Beyond All Praising

1. O God be-yond all prais - ing, we wor-ship you to -
day and sing the love a - maz - ing that
songs can - not re - pay; for we can on - ly
won - der at ev - ery gift you send, at
bless - ings with - out num - ber and mer - cies with - out
end: We lift our hearts be - fore you and
wait up - on your Word, we hon - or and a -
dore you, our great and might - y Lord.

2. Then hear, O gra-cious Sav - ior, ac - cept the love we
bring, that we who know your fa - vor may
serve you as our king; and whe - ther our to -
mor - rows be filled with good or ill, we'll
tri - umph through our sor - rows and rise to bless you
still: To mar - vel at your beau - ty and
glo - ry in your ways, and make a joy - ful
du - ty our sac - ri - fice of praise.

WORDS: Michael Perry (Heb. 13:15)
MUSIC: Gustav T. Holst

THAXTED
13 13.13 13.13 13

2010
I Am Who I Am,
I Will Be Who I Will

1. "I am who I am, I will be who I will,
2. "I am who I am!" now in this time and place.
3. "I am who I am!"— God both faith-ful and free;
4. God's names are so var-ied: Rock, Ea-gle, and Dove,

un-fet-tered Cre-a-tor and cre-a-ting still!"
God with us! Christ with us! the full-ness of grace!
un-bound by tra-di-tion, "I'll be who I'll be."
Mes-si-ah, Em-man-u-el, Wis-dom, and Love.

In such words of free-dom, our God's clar-ion voice
Each day is ex-cit-ing, with jus-tice our goal,
"I will be who I will be"— God be-yond thought,
Yet all are re-flec-tions of on-ly a part.

speaks loud-ly or soft-ly, and our hearts re-joice.
the Spir-it ig-nit-ing new flames in the soul.
un-shack-led by an-y-thing peo-ple have wrought.
"I will be who I will be"— that is the heart!

WORDS: Jane Parker Huber (Exod. 3:13-14)
MUSIC: Welsh folk melody
Words © 1996 Jane Parker Huber

ST. DENIO
11 11.11 11

We Sing of Your Glory
(Tuya Es la Gloria)

1. We sing of your glo - ry, we praise you a - gain,
2. We sing of your pow - er and hon - or a - gain,
1. *Tu - ya es la glo - ria la hon - ra tam - bién;*
2. *Tu - yos los do - mi - nios, los tro - nos tam - bién;*

for you are e - ter - nal. A - men. A - men.
for you are e - ter - nal. A - men. A - men.
tu - ya pa - ra siem - pre. A - mén. A - mén.
tu - yos pa - ra siem - pre. A - mén. A - mén.

3. We sing of surrender
to you, God, again.
Your power is eternal. Amen. Amen.

4. "Glory in the highest,
on earth," sing again.
Glory, alleluia. Amen. Amen.

3. *A ti yo me rindo,*
te adoro también;
amor absoluto. Amén. Amén.

4. *Gloria en las alturas*
y en la tierra también;
gloria, aleluya. Amén. Amén.

WORDS: Trad. Latin American; English trans. by S. T. Kimbrough Jr. (Deut. 32:11, 18;
33:27; Ps. 57:1; 66:2; 96:1-2)
MUSIC: Trad. Latin American; harm. by Carlton R. Young

RÍO DE LA PLATA
65.64

English trans. and harm. © 1996 General Board of Global Ministries, GBGMusik

2012   Let Us with a Joyful Mind

1. Let us with a joy - ful mind praise our
2. New - made earth was filled with light through God's
3. Daz - zling bright the sun o - beys God who
4. Stars and moon that span - gle night all de -
5. Crea - tures of the sea and land all are
6. There - fore with a joy - ful mind, praise our

Refrain

God for - ev - er kind,
all com-mand - ing might,
shines with bright - er rays, } rich with mer - cies that en -
pend on heav - en's light,
fed by God's own hand,
God for - ev - er kind,

dure, ev - er faith - ful, ev - er sure.

WORDS: John Milton, adapt. by Thomas H. Troeger (Ps. 136)   INNOCENTS
MUSIC: From *The Parish Choir* (1850)   77.77
Words adapt. © 1995 Oxford University Press, Inc.

Bless the Lord

Bless the Lord my soul and bless God's ho - ly name.

Bless the Lord my soul who leads me in - to life.

WORDS: Jacques Berthier (Ps. 103:1)
MUSIC: Jacques Berthier and the Taizé Community

BLESS THE LORD (TAIZÉ)
Irregular

© 1984 Les Presses de Taizé (France). Used by permission of GIA Publications, Inc.

Alleluia

Al - le - lu - ia, al - le - lu - ia, al - le - lu - ia.

Al - le - lu - ia, al - le - lu - ia, al - le - lu - ia.

TAIZÉ ALLELUIA
Irregular

MUSIC: Jacques Berthier

© 1982, 1983, 1984 Les Presses de Taizé (France). Used by permission of GIA Publications, Inc.

2015   Bless His Holy Name

Bless the Lord,   O my soul,   and   all   that is   with-

Fine

in me, bless his   ho - ly   name.

He has done great things,   he has done great   things,

D.C. al Fine

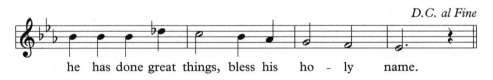

he has done great things, bless his   ho - ly   name.

WORDS: Andraé Crouch (Ps. 103:1)   BLESS HIS HOLY NAME
MUSIC: Andraé Crouch   Irregular

2016   Glorify Thy Name

1. Fa - ther,
2. Je - sus, } we love you, we wor - ship and a - dore you,
3. Spir - it,

glo - ri - fy thy name in all the earth. _____

WORDS: Donna Adkins (Ps. 86:12)   GLORIFY THY NAME
MUSIC: Donna Adkins   Irregular

Glo - ri - fy thy name, glo - ri - fy thy name,

glo - ri - fy thy name in all the earth. _____

Come, Rejoice in God

(Jubilate Servite)

2017

① Come, re - joice in God; praise him all the earth.
Ju - bi - la - te De - o om - nis ter - ra,

② Serve your God, serve your God, glad - ly serve your God!
ser - vi - te Do - mi - no in lae - ti - ti - a,

③ Hal - le - lu - jah, hal - le - lu - jah, glad - ly serve your God;
Al - le - lu - ia, al - le - lu - ia, in lae - ti - ti - a!

④ hal - le - lu - jah, hal - le - lu - jah, glad - ly serve your God!
Al - le - lu - ia, al - le - lu - ia, in lae - ti - ti - a!

May be sung as a round.

WORDS: Jacques Berthier (Ps. 100) JUBILATE SERVITE
MUSIC: Jacques Berthier Irregular

2018   Honor and Praise

1. Righ-teous and ho - ly in all of your ways;
2. Fill - ing the tem - ple, the work of your grace;

we come be - fore you with hon - or and praise.

Here to a - dore you for all of our days,

we come be - fore you with hon - or and praise. _____

Lord of the heav - ens, how faith - ful you are.

Shine down up - on us, } O bright Morn-ing Star. _____
Rise in our spir - its, }

Righ-teous and ho - ly in all of your ways;

we come be - fore you with hon - or and praise.

WORDS: Twila Paris (Rev. 22:16)   HONOR AND PRAISE
MUSIC: Twila Paris   Irregular

Holy
(Santo)

Ho - ly, ho - ly, ho - ly, ho - ly, ho - ly, ho - ly is our
ho - ly, ho - ly, ho - ly, ho - ly, ho - ly is our
San - to, san - to, san - to, san - to, san - to, san - to es nues - tro
san - to, san - to, san - to, san - to, san - to es nues - tro

Lord, God is Lord of all cre - a - tion, ho - ly,
Lord, God is Lord of past and fu - ture, ho - ly,
Dios, Se - ñor de to - da la tie - rra, san - to,
Dios, Se - ñor de to - da la his - to - ria, san - to,

1
ho - ly is our Lord.
ho - ly is our
san - to es nues - tro Dios.
san - to es nues - tro

2
Ho - ly,
Lord.
San - to,
Dios.

In the mid - dle of the vill - age, be -
Bless - ings to the one who teach - es the
Que a - com - pa - ña a nues - tro pue - blo, que
Ben - di - tos los que en su nom - bre el

side us in our strug - gles, through - out the whole cre -
good news of the Gos - pel, the mes - sage of sal -
vi - ve en nues - tras lu - chas, del u - ni - ver - so en -
e - van - ge - lio a - nun - cian, la bue - na y gran no -

1
a - tion, God is the on - ly One.
va - tion, of peace and lib - er -
te - ro el ú - ni - co Se - ñor.
ti - cia de la li - be - ra -

2
ty.
ción.

WORDS: Guillermo Cuéllar from *La Misa Popular Salvadoreña*;
        English trans. by Josué Alvarez and Debi Tyree (Isa. 6:3)
MUSIC: Guillermo Cuéllar from *La Misa Popular Salvadoreña*

CUÉLLAR
87.87 D 87.87 D

2020   Praise the Lord with the Sound of Trumpet

1. Praise the Lord with the sound of trum - pet,
2. Praise the Lord with the crash - ing cym - bal,

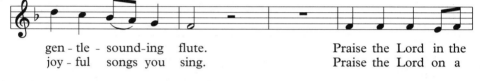

praise the Lord with the harp and lute, praise the Lord with the
praise the Lord with the pipe and string, praise the Lord with the

gen - tle - sound-ing flute.   Praise the Lord in the
joy - ful songs you sing.   Praise the Lord on a

field and for - est, praise the Lord in the cit - y square,
week - day morn - ing, praise the Lord on a Sun - day noon,

praise the Lord an - y - time and an - y - where.
praise the Lord by the light of sun or moon.

Praise the Lord in the wind and sun-shine, praise the Lord in the
Praise the Lord in the time of sor - row, praise the Lord in the

dark of night, praise the Lord in the rain or snow or
time of joy, praise the Lord ev - ery mo - ment; noth - ing

May be sung as a canon.

WORDS: Natalie Sleeth (Ps. 150)
MUSIC: Natalie Sleeth

PRAISE THE LORD
Irregular

in the morn-ing light. Praise the Lord in the
let your praise de-stroy. Praise the Lord in the

deep-est val-ley, praise the Lord on the high-est hill,
peace and qui-et, praise the Lord in your work or play,

praise the Lord; nev-er let your voice be still.
praise the Lord ev-ery-where in ev-ery way!

What a Mighty God We Serve 2021

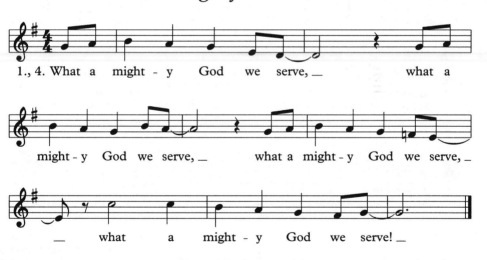

1., 4. What a might-y God we serve, ___ what a

might-y God we serve, ___ what a might-y God we serve, ___

___ what a might-y God we serve! ___

2. Let us sing and praise the Lord …
3. Let us shout and praise God's name …

WORDS: Trad. African folk song; adapt. by Jack Schrader   MIGHTY GOD
MUSIC: Trad. African folk song; adapt. by Jack Schrader   Irregular

Adapt. © 1995 Hope Publishing Co.

2022   Great Is the Lord

Refrain

Great is the Lord, he is ho-ly and just; by his

pow-er we trust in his love. Great is the Lord, he is

faith-ful and true; by his mer-cy he proves he is love.

1., 2. Great is the Lord and wor-thy of glo-ry! Great is the Lord and
3. Great are you, Lord, and wor-thy of glo-ry! Great are you, Lord, and

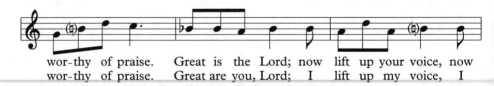

wor-thy of praise. Great is the Lord; now lift up your voice, now
wor-thy of praise. Great are you, Lord; I lift up my voice, I

lift up your voice: Great _____ is the Lord! _____
lift up my voice: Great _____ are you, Lord! _____

First time D.C.
Second time D.S.

_____ Great _____ is the Lord!
_____ Great _____ are you, Lord!

WORDS: Michael W. Smith and Deborah D. Smith (Ps. 35:27)
MUSIC: Michael W. Smith and Deborah D. Smith

GREAT IS THE LORD
Irregular with Refrain

How Majestic Is Your Name

2023

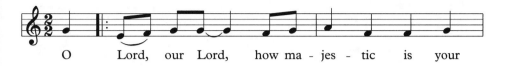

O Lord, our Lord, how ma - jes - tic is your

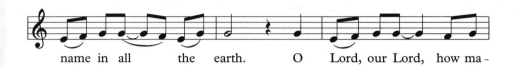

name in all the earth. O Lord, our Lord, how ma -

jes - tic is your name in all the earth. O

Lord, _____ we praise your name. O

Lord, _____ we mag - ni - fy your name: Prince of

Peace, might - y God; O Lord God Al -

Repeat ending | *Song ending*

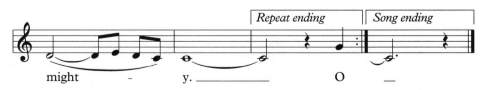

might - y. _____ O _____

WORDS: Michael W. Smith (Ps. 8:1, 9; Isa. 9:6)
MUSIC: Michael W. Smith

HOW MAJESTIC
Irregular

2024 From the Rising of the Sun

From the ris - ing of the sun ___ to the go-ing down of the same, _ the name of the Lord shall be praised. ___ From the ris - ing of the sun _ to the go-ing down of the same, _ _ the name of the Lord shall be praised. ___ So praise ye the Lord. ___ Praise ye the Lord. ___ From the ris - ing of the sun _

WORDS: Anon. (Ps. 113:3)
MUSIC: Anon.

RISING SUN
Irregular

to the go-ing down of the same, — the

name of the Lord shall be praised. _____

As the Deer

2025

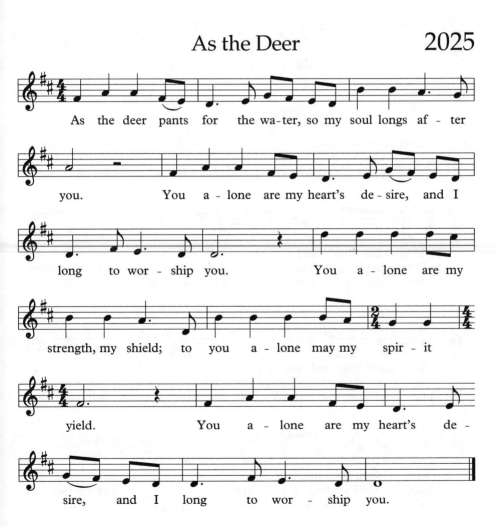

As the deer pants for the wa-ter, so my soul longs af - ter

you. You a - lone are my heart's de - sire, and I

long to wor - ship you. You a - lone are my

strength, my shield; to you a - lone may my spir - it

yield. You a - lone are my heart's de -

sire, and I long to wor - ship you.

WORDS: Martin J. Nystrom (Ps. 42:1)
MUSIC: Martin J. Nystrom

AS THE DEER
Irregular

2026 Halle, Halle, Halleluja

Hal-le, Hal-le, Hal - le - lu - ja! Hal-le, Hal-le, Hal -

le - lu - ja! Hal - le, Hal - le, Hal - le -

lu - ja! Hal-le - lu-ja! Hal - le - lu - ja!

WORDS: Trad. Caribbean
MUSIC: Trad. Caribbean

HALLE, HALLE
Irregular

2027 Now Praise the Hidden God of Love

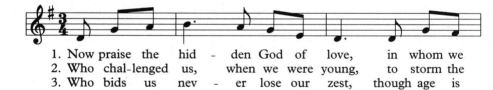

1. Now praise the hid - den God of love, in whom we
2. Who chal-lenged us, when we were young, to storm the
3. Who bids us nev - er lose our zest, though age is

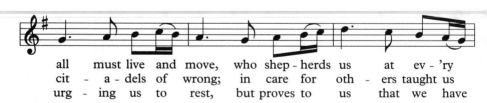

all must live and move, who shep-herds us at ev - 'ry
cit - a-dels of wrong; in care for oth - ers taught us
urg - ing us to rest, but proves to us that we have

stage, through youth, ma - tur - i - ty, and age:
how God's true com - mun - i - ty must grow:
still a work to do, a place to fill.

WORDS: Fred Pratt Green (Acts 17:23-28)
MUSIC: English folk melody

O WALY WALY
LM

Clap Your Hands

WORDS: Handt Hanson and Paul Murakami (Ps. 47:1)
MUSIC: Handt Hanson and Paul Murakami

CLAP YOUR HANDS
Irregular

2029   Praise to the Lord

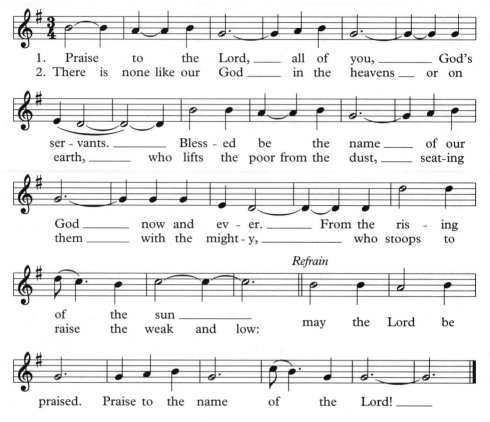

1. Praise to the Lord, ___ all of you, ___ God's
2. There is none like our God ___ in the heavens ___ or on

ser - vants. ___ Bless - ed be the name ___ of our
earth, ___ who lifts the poor from the dust, ___ seat-ing

God ___ now and ev - er. ___ From the ris - ing
them ___ with the might - y, ___ who stoops to

Refrain

of the sun ___ may the Lord be
raise the weak and low:

praised. Praise to the name of the Lord! ___

WORDS: Ron Klusmeier (Ps. 113)
MUSIC: Ron Klusmeier

RICHARDSON-BURTON
Irregular with Refrain

© 1972 Ron Klusmeier. Reprinted with permission of MUSIKLUS.

2030   The First Song of Isaiah

Refrain

Sure - ly, it is God who saves me; I will

trust in him and not be a - fraid. For the

Stanzas included in other editions.

WORDS: From *The Book of Common Prayer,* Canticle 9 (Isa. 12:2-6)
MUSIC: Jack Noble White

FIRST SONG
Irregular

© 1976 Belwin-Mills Publishing Corp. (admin. by Warner Bros. Publications)

Lord is my strong-hold and my sure de-fense, and

he will be my Sav - ior. _____

We Bring the Sacrifice of Praise 2031

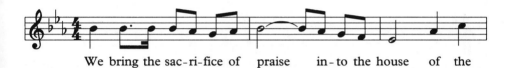

We bring the sac-ri-fice of praise in-to the house of the

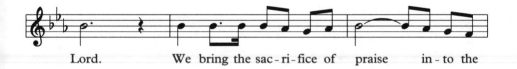

Lord. We bring the sac-ri-fice of praise in-to the

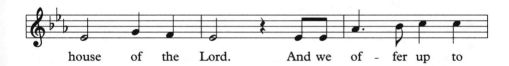

house of the Lord. And we of - fer up to

you the sac-ri - fic - es of thanks-giv - ing; and we

of - fer up to you the sac-ri - fic - es of joy.

WORDS: Kirk Dearman (Heb. 13:15)　　　　　　　　　　SACRIFICE OF PRAISE
MUSIC: Kirk Dearman　　　　　　　　　　　　　　　　Irregular

2032 My Life Is in You, Lord

My life is in you, Lord; my strength is in you, Lord; my hope is in you, Lord; in you, it's in you. My life is in you, Lord; my strength is in you, Lord; my hope is in

Second time to Coda

you, Lord; in you, it's in you. I will praise you with all of my life, _____ I will praise you with all of my strength; _____ with all of my life, with all of my strength.

WORDS: Daniel Gardner
MUSIC: Daniel Gardner

MY LIFE
Irregular

D.S. al Coda

All of my hope is in you. _____ My

CODA

you, it's in you, in you. _____

Glory to God

(Gloria a Dios)

2033

1. Glo-ry to God, glo-ry to God, glo-ry in the high-est!
2. Glo-ry to God, glo-ry to God, glo-ry to Christ Je-sus!
3. Glo-ry to God, glo-ry to God, glo-ry to the Spir-it!

1. ¡Glo-ria a Dios, glo-ria a Dios, glo-ria en los cie-los!
2. ¡Glo-ria a Dios, glo-ria a Dios, glo-ria a Je-su-cris-to!
3. ¡Glo-ria a Dios, glo-ria a Dios, glo-ria al Es-pí-ri-tu!

To God be glo-ry for-ev-er!	
To God be glo-ry for-ev-er!	Al-le-lu-ia, A-men!
To God be glo-ry for-ev-er!	

¡A Dios la glo-ria por siem-pre!	
¡A Dios la glo-ria por siem-pre!	¡A-le-lu-ya, A-mén!
¡A Dios la glo-ria por siem-pre!	

Al-le-lu-ia, A-men! Al-le-lu-ia, A-men! _____

¡A-le-lu-ya, A-mén! ¡A-le-lu-ya, A-mén! _____

May be sung in call and response pattern.

WORDS: Trad. Peruvian (Luke 2:14)
MUSIC: Trad. Peruvian

MACHU-PICHU
Irregular

2034 Blessed Be the Name of the Lord

1., 4. Bless-ed be the name of the Lord, ___
bless-ed be the name of the Lord, _____
bless-ed be the name of the Lord ___ most ___ high. ___
___ Bless-ed be the name of the Lord, ___
___ bless-ed be the name of the Lord, _____

Fourth time to Coda ⊕ | 1, 3

bless-ed be the name of the Lord ___ most ___ high. ___

| 2

___ ___ most ___ high. ___

The name of the Lord ___ is ___ a strong tow-

2. Glory to the name of the Lord ...
3. Holy is the name of the Lord ...

WORDS: Clinton Utterbach (Prov. 18:10)   UTTERBACH
MUSIC: Clinton Utterbach   Irregular

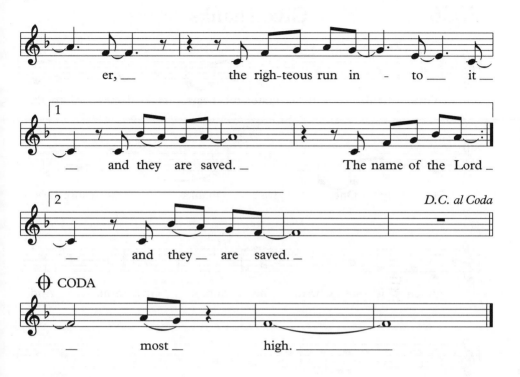

er, ___ the righ-teous run in - to ___ it ___

1 ___ and they are saved. ___ The name of the Lord ___

2 ___ and they ___ are saved. ___

D.C. al Coda

CODA ___ most ___ high. _____

Praise, Praise, Praise the Lord   2035

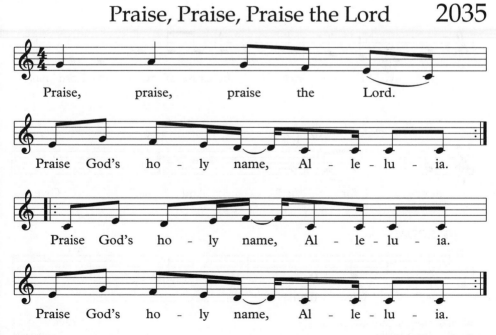

Praise, praise, praise the Lord.

Praise God's ho - ly name, Al - le - lu - ia.

Praise God's ho - ly name, Al - le - lu - ia.

Praise God's ho - ly name, Al - le - lu - ia.

WORDS: Trad. Cameroon
MUSIC: Trad. Cameroon
AFRICAN PROCESSIONAL
Irregular
© 1994 Earthsongs

2036   Give Thanks

Give thanks with a grate-ful heart, give thanks to the

Ho - ly One, give thanks be-cause he's

giv-en Je - sus Christ his Son. Give Son. And

now let the weak say, "I am strong"; let the

poor say, "I am rich be-cause of what the Lord has

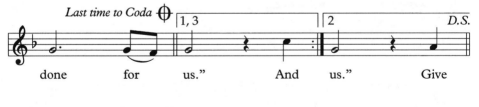

Last time to Coda

done for us." And us." Give

CODA

us." Give thanks!

WORDS: Henry Smith (Luke 1:49-53)
MUSIC: Henry Smith

GIVE THANKS
Irregular

© 1978 Integrity's Hosanna! Music

I Sing Praises to Your Name

2037

1. I sing prais-es to your name, O

Lord, prais-es to your name, O Lord, for your

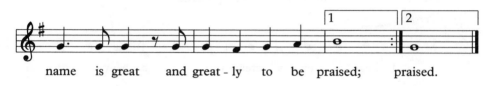

name is great and great-ly to be praised; praised.

2. I give glory to your name ...

WORDS: Terry MacAlmon (Ps. 7:17; 9:2; 48:1; 96:4; 145:3)
MUSIC: Terry MacAlmon

© 1988 Integrity's Hosanna! Music

I SING PRAISES
Irregular

Father, I Adore You

2038

1. Fa - ther, I a - dore you, lay my life be -

fore you; how I love you.

2. Jesus, I adore you ...
3. Spirit, I adore you ...

May be sung as a canon.

WORDS: Terrye Coehlo Strom (Matt. 6:9)
MUSIC: Terrye Coehlo Strom

MARANATHA
66.4

© 1972 CCM Music (admin. by Maranatha! Music c/o The Copyright Co., Nashville, TN)

2039 Blessing and Honor

Chorus

To the one seat-ed on the throne and to the

Repeat ending

Lamb, all bless-ing and hon - or, glo - ry and might.

Song ending

or, glo - ry and might. __

Verse

I heard ev - er - y crea - ture in heav-en and on

earth sing-ing prais-es to God. I heard ev-er-y crea-

D.C.

ture in the sea sing-ing prais-es to God. _

WORDS: Chip Andrus (Rev. 4-5)
MUSIC: Chip Andrus

BLESSING AND HONOR
Irregular

2040 Awesome God

Our God is an awe - some God; he

reigns from heav-en a - bove with wis - dom,

WORDS: Rich Mullins (Deut. 10:17; Ps. 33:8; Matt. 13:54; Mark 6:2; Rev. 5:12; 19:6-7)
MUSIC: Rich Mullins

AWESOME GOD
Irregular

pow'r, and love. Our God is an awe - some God!

Thou Art Worthy 2041

Thou art wor - thy, thou art wor - thy, thou art

wor - thy, O Lord, _____ to re-ceive glo - ry,

glo - ry and hon - or, glo - ry and hon - or and

power. _____ For thou hast cre - at - ed, hast

all things cre - at - ed; thou hast cre - at - ed all

things. _____ And for thy plea - sure they are cre -

at - ed; thou art wor - thy, O Lord. _____

WORDS: Pauline Michael Mills (Rev. 4:11)
MUSIC: Pauline Michael Mills

WORTHY
Irregular

2042   I Believe in God Almighty

1. I be - lieve in God al - might-y, Fa - ther of all
2. I be - lieve that Je - sus suf-fered, scourged and scorned and
3. I be - lieve in God's own Spir - it, bond - ing all the

things that be, Mak - er of the earth and heav-ens,
cru - ci - fied; tak - en from the cross, was bur-ied—
saints with - in one Church, cath - o - lic and ho - ly,

Keep - er of the sky and sea. I be - lieve in
True Life there had tru - ly died. I be - lieve that
where for - give - ness frees from sin; in the bod - y's

God's Son, Je - sus, now for us both Lord and Christ, of the
on the third day Christ was raised up from the grave, then as -
res - ur - rec - tion, for the break-ing of death's chain gives the

Spir - it and of Mar - y born to bring a - bun - dant life.
cend-ed to God's right hand. He will come to judge and save.
life that's ev - er - last - ing. This the faith that I have claimed.

WORDS: Sylvia G. Dunstan
MUSIC: Adapt. from a Welsh melody
Words © 1991 GIA Publications, Inc.

ARFON (Major)
87.87 D

2043   Alleluia

Al - le - lu - ia! Al - le - lu - ia!

Stanzas included in other editions.

MUSIC: Fintan O'Carroll and Christopher Walker
© 1985 Fintan O'Carroll and Christopher Walker. Pub. by OCP Publications

CELTIC ALLELUIA
Irregular

Al - le - lu - ia! Al - le - lu - ia!

My Gratitude Now Accept, O God 2044
(Gracias, Señor)

1. My grat - i - tude now ac - cept, O God, for ten - der
2. From all your boun - ty I give to you; for all the
1. Gra - cias, Se - ñor, por lo que me das, gra - cias por
2. Te doy de lo que tú me das, con go - zo

care that you pro - vide; for your a - bun - dant
bless - ings you im - part. Re - ceive this of - fer -
ben - de - cir - me. Gra - cias por tu fi -
en mi co - ra - zón. Re - ci - be hoy mi o -

1-3

faith - ful - ness. End - less is your sup - ply. _____
ing I bring. Re - ceive my joy - ful heart. _____
de - li - dad y por tu pro - vi - sión. _____
fren - da, te la en - tre - go a ti. _____

4

gifts from the heart ac - cept. _____
de lo que tú nos das. _____

3. I bring to you all my love and praise.
   I glorify and bless your name.
   Let me adore you, Holy One,
   with every breath I take.

3. Te amo, Dios, doy gloria a ti,
   tú eres digno de loor.
   Te adoro con mi vida
   y con lo que me das.

4. All that is living belongs to you;
   all that I am in your hands kept.
   From the abundance of your hand,
   gifts from the heart accept.

4. Todo te pertenece a ti,
   mi vida y todo mi ser.
   Con gratitud te damos
   de lo que tú nos das.

WORDS: Rafael Montalvo; English trans. by Raquel Mora Martínez (Ps. 24:1)
MUSIC: Rafael Montalvo

OFRENDA
Irregular

Trans. © 1999 Abingdon Press (admin. by The Copyright Co., Nashville, TN)

2045   Sing a New Song to the Lord

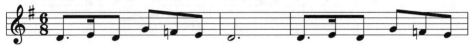

1. Sing   a   new song to   the   Lord,   he   to whom won-ders be -
2. Now   to   the ends of the earth   see his sal - va - tion is
3. Sing   a   new song and re - joice,   pub - lish his prais - es   a -
4. Join with the hills and the sea   thun-ders of praise to pro -

long!   Re - joice   in   his   tri - umph   and
shown!   And   still   he   re - mem - bers   his
broad!   Let   voic - es   in   cho - rus,   with
long!   In   judg-ment   and   jus - tice   he

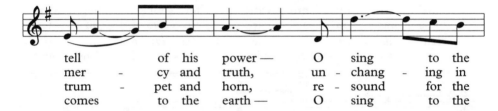

tell   of   his   power —   O   sing   to   the
mer   -   cy and   truth,   un - chang - ing   in
trum -   pet and   horn,   re - sound   for   the
comes   to   the   earth —   O   sing   to   the

Lord   a   new   song!
love   to   his   own.
joy   of   the   Lord!
Lord   a   new   song!

WORDS: Timothy Dudley-Smith (Ps. 98)   ONSLOW SQUARE
MUSIC: David G. Wilson   77.11 8

Words © 1973 Hope Publishing Co.; music © 1973 Jubilee Hymns (admin. by Hope Publishing Co.)

PRAISE AND THANKSGIVING, *see further:*

Womb of Life

1. Womb of life, and source of be - ing, home of
2. Word in flesh, our broth - er Je - sus, born to
3. Brood-ing Spir - it, move a - mong us; be our
4. Moth - er, Broth - er, Ho - ly Part - ner; Fa - ther,

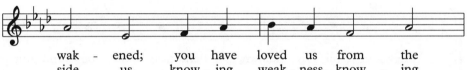

ev - ery rest - less heart, in your arms the worlds a -
bring us sec - ond birth, you have come to stand be -
part-ner, be our friend. When our mem - ory fails, re -
Spir - it, On - ly Son: We would praise your name for -

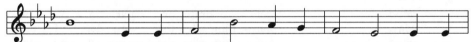

wak - ened; you have loved us from the
side us, know - ing weak - ness, know - ing
mind us whose we are, what we in -
ev - er, One - in - three, and Three - in -

start. We, your chil - dren, gath - er 'round you, at the
earth. Priest who shares our hu - man strug - gles, Life of
tend. La - bor with us, aid the birth - ing of the
one. We would share your life, your pas - sion, share your

ta - ble you pre - pare. Shar-ing stor - ies, tears, and
Life, and Death of Death, Ris - en Christ, come stand a -
new world yet to be, free of ser - vant, lord, and
word of world made new, ev - er sing - ing, ev - er

laugh - ter, we are nur-tured by your care.
mong us, send the Spir - it by your breath.
mas - ter, free for love and u - ni - ty.
prais - ing, one with all, and one with you.

WORDS: Ruth Duck (John 1:14; 20:19-23)
MUSIC: Skinner Chávez-Melo

RAQUEL
87.87 D

Words © 1992 GIA Publications, Inc.; music © 1985, 1991 Skinner Chávez-Melo

2047   Bring Many Names

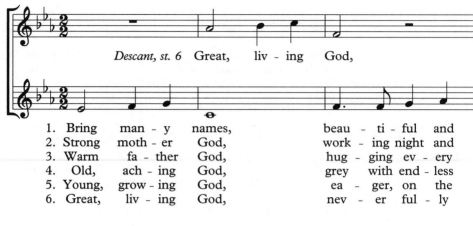

Descant, st. 6   Great, liv-ing God,

1. Bring man - y names,   beau - ti - ful and
2. Strong moth - er God,   work - ing night and
3. Warm fa - ther God,   hug - ging ev - ery
4. Old, ach - ing God,   grey with end - less
5. Young, grow - ing God,   ea - ger, on the
6. Great, liv - ing God,   nev - er ful - ly

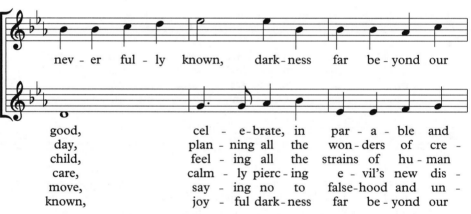

nev - er ful - ly known, dark - ness far be - yond our

good,   cel - e-brate, in par - a - ble and
day,   plan - ning all the won - ders of cre -
child,   feel - ing all the strains of hu - man
care,   calm - ly pierc - ing e - vil's new dis -
move,   say - ing no to false-hood and un -
known,   joy - ful dark - ness far be - yond our

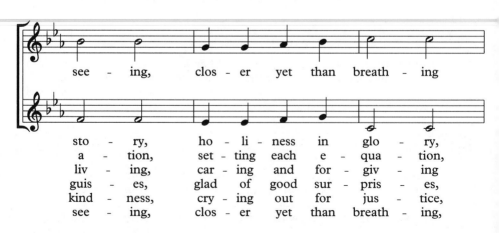

see - ing, clos - er yet than breath - ing

sto - ry, ho - li - ness in glo - ry,
a - tion, set - ting each e - qua - tion,
liv - ing, car - ing and for - giv - ing
guis - es, glad of good sur - pris - es,
kind - ness, cry - ing out for jus - tice,
see - ing, clos - er yet than breath - ing,

WORDS: Brian Wren
MUSIC: Carlton R. Young

WESTCHASE
9 10.11 9

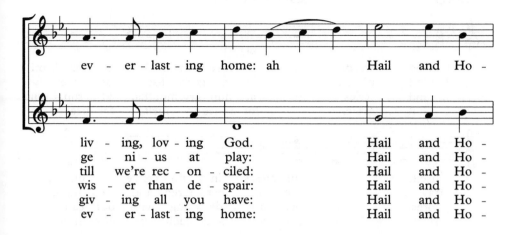

ev - er - last - ing home: ah   Hail   and   Ho -

liv - ing, lov - ing God.   Hail   and   Ho -
ge - ni - us   at   play: Hail   and   Ho -
till   we're rec - on - ciled: Hail   and   Ho -
wis - er   than de - spair: Hail   and   Ho -
giv - ing   all   you   have: Hail   and   Ho -
ev - er - last - ing   home: Hail   and   Ho -

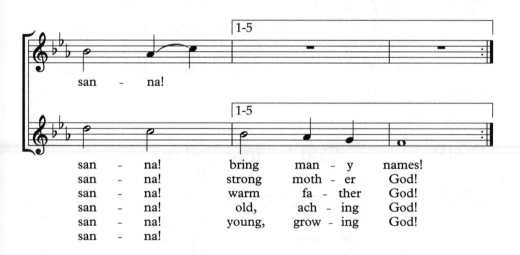

1-5

san - na!

1-5

san - na!   bring   man - y   names!
san - na!   strong   moth - er   God!
san - na!   warm   fa - ther   God!
san - na!   old,   ach - ing   God!
san - na!   young,   grow - ing   God!
san - na!

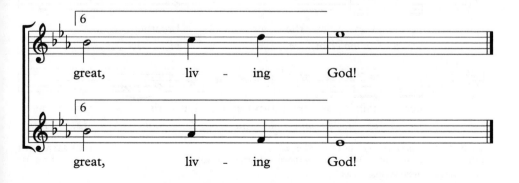

6

great,   liv - ing   God!

6

great,   liv - ing   God!

2048 God Weeps

1. God weeps at love with-held, at strength mis-
2. God bleeds at an-ger's fist, at trust be-
3. God cries at hun-gry mouths, at run-ning
4. God waits for stones to melt, for peace to

used, at chil-dren's in-no-cence a-bused,
trayed, at wom-en bat-tered and a-fraid,
sores, at crea-tures dy-ing with-out cause,
seed, for hearts to hold each oth-er's need,

and till we change the way we love, God weeps.
and till we change the way we win, God bleeds.
and till we change the way we care, God cries.
and till we un-der-stand the Christ, God waits.

WORDS: Shirley Erena Murray
MUSIC: Carlton R. Young

HIROSHIMA
64.8 10

© 1996 Hope Publishing Co.

2049 God Is Here Today
(Dios Está Aquí)

God is here to-day; _____ as
Dios es-tá a-quí, _____ tan

cer-tain as the air I breathe, _____ as
cier-to co-mo el ai-re que res-pi-ro, _____ tan

cer-tain as the morn-ing sun that ris-es, as
cier-to co-mo la ma-ña-na se le-van-ta, tan

WORDS: Trad. Mexican; trans. by C. Michael Hawn
MUSIC: Trad. Mexican; arr. by C. Michael Hawn and Arturo González

DIOS ESTÁ AQUÍ
Irregular

Trans. and arr. © 1999 Choristers Guild

cer - tain when I sing you'll hear my song. _____
cier - to co - mo que le can-to y me pue-de o - ir. _____

Mothering God, You Gave Me Birth 2050

1. Moth-er-ing God, you gave me birth in the bright
2. Moth-er-ing Christ, you took my form, of - fer - ing
3. Moth-er-ing Spir - it, nur - t'ring one, in arms of

morn - ing of this world. Cre - at - or, source of
me your food of light, grain of life, and
pa - tience hold me close, so that in faith I

ev - ery breath, you are my rain, my wind, my sun.
grape of love, your ver - y bod - y for my peace.
root and grow un - til I flow'r, un - til I know.

WORDS: Jean Janzen, based on the writings of Juliana of Norwich (15th cent.)   MARYTON
MUSIC: H. Percy Smith   LM

2051

I Was There to Hear
Your Borning Cry

1. I was there to hear your born - ing cry, I'll be
3. When you heard the won - der of the Word, I was
5. In the mid – dle ag - es of your life, not too
7. I was there to hear your born - ing cry, I'll be

there when you are old. I re - joiced the day you
there to cheer you on. You were raised to praise the
old, no long - er young, I'll be there to guide you
there when you are old, I re - joiced the day you

were bap - tized to see your life un - fold.
liv - ing Lord to whom you now be - long.
through the night, com - plete what I've be - gun.
were bap - tized to see your life un - fold.

Fine

2. I was there when you were but a child with a
4. If you find some-one to share your time and you
6. When the eve - ning gent - ly clos - es in and you

faith to suit you well; in a blaze of light you
join your hearts as one, I'll be there to make your
shut your wea - ry eyes, I'll be there as I have

D.C.

wan - dered off to find where de - mons dwell.
vers - es rhyme from dusk till ris - ing sun.
al - ways been with just one more sur - prise.

WORDS: John Ylvisaker
MUSIC: John Ylvisaker

WATERLIFE
97.96 D

© 1985 John C. Ylvisaker

The Lone, Wild Bird

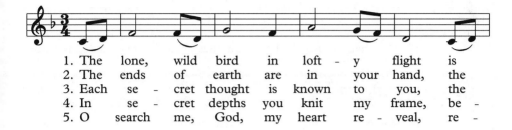

1. The lone, wild bird in loft - y flight is
2. The ends of earth are in your hand, the
3. Each se - cret thought is known to you, the
4. In se - cret depths you knit my frame, be -
5. O search me, God, my heart re - veal, re -

still with you, nor leaves your sight. And
sea's dark deep and far - off land. And
path I walk my whole life through; my
fore my birth you spoke my name; with -
new my life, my spir - it heal; for

I am yours! I rest in you, Great
I am yours! I rest in you, Great
days, my deeds, my hopes, my fears, my
in my soul, as close as breath, so
I am yours, I rest in you, Great

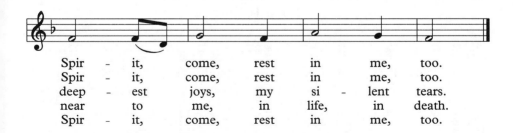

Spir - it, come, rest in me, too.
Spir - it, come, rest in me, too.
deep - est joys, my si - lent tears.
near to me, in life, in death.
Spir - it, come, rest in me, too.

WORDS: Sts. 1-3 by Henry Richard McFayden, alt.; sts. 4-5 by Marty Haugen (Ps. 139:2-4,
 13-15, 23-24)
MUSIC: Walker's *Southern Harmony* (1835)

PROSPECT
LM

Sts. 4-5 © 1991 GIA Publications, Inc.

2053 If It Had Not Been for the Lord

Refrain

If it had not been for the Lord on my side, tell me where would I be, _____ where would I be. If it

1 *Fine*

be.

2

be.
1. He kept my en-e-mies a-way; he let the
2. He nev-er left me all a-lone; he gave the

sun shine through a cloud-y day. He
peace and joy I'd nev-er known. He

rocked me in the cra-dle of his arm when he
an-swered when I knelt to real-ly pray, and in

D.S. al Fine

knew I had been bat-tered and scorned, so if it
vic-t'ry the Lord brought me his way, so if it

WORDS: Margaret P. Douroux
MUSIC: Margaret P. Douroux

WHERE WOULD I BE
Irregular with Refrain

© 1980 Margaret P. Douroux

2054 Nothing Can Trouble
(Nada Te Turbe)

Noth-ing can trou-ble, noth-ing can fright-en.
Na-da te tur-be, na-da te es-pan-te.

WORDS: St. Teresa de Jesús; Taizé Community
MUSIC: Jacques Berthier

NADA TE TURBE
Irregular

© 1991 Les Presses de Taizé (France). Used by permission of GIA Publications, Inc.

Those who seek God shall nev-er go want-ing.
Quien a Dios tie - ne na - da le fal - ta.

God a - lone fills us.
So - lo Dios bas - ta.

You Are My Hiding Place 2055

You are my hid - ing place. You al - ways

fill my heart with songs of de - liv - er-ance, when-ev-er I am a -

fraid, I will trust in you, I will trust in

you. Let the weak say, "I am strong in the

Repeat ending | *Song ending*

strength of the Lord." Lord. I will trust in you."

May be sung as a canon.

WORDS: Michael Ledner (Ps. 32:7)
MUSIC: Michael Ledner

HIDING PLACE
Irregular

© 1981 CCCM Music (admin. by Maranatha! Music c/o The Copyright Co., Nashville, TN)

2056 God Is So Good

1. God is so good, God is so good,
2. God cares for me, God cares for me,
3. God loves me so, God loves me so,
4. God is so good, God is so good,

God is so good, }
God cares for me, }
God loves me so, } God's so good to me.
God is so good, }

WORDS: Trad.
MUSIC: Trad.

GOD IS SO GOOD
Irregular

2057 Be Still and Know That I Am God

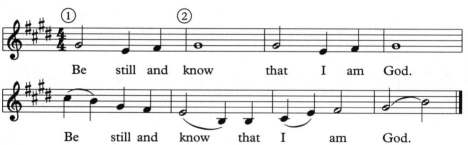

Be still and know that I am God.

Be still and know that I am God.

May be sung as a canon.
WORDS: John Bell (Ps. 46)
MUSIC: John Bell

PSALM 46
Irregular

2058 Shepherd Me, O God

Shep-herd me, O God, be - yond my wants, be -

yond my fears, from death in - to life. _____

Stanzas included in other editions.
WORDS: Marty Haugen (Ps. 23)
MUSIC: Marty Haugen

SHEPHERD ME
Irregular

PROVIDENCE, *see further:*
2218 You Are Mine

I Am Your Mother
(Earth Prayer)

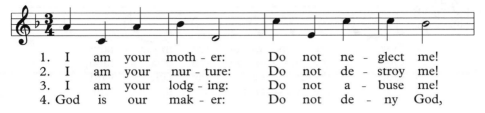

1. I am your moth-er: Do not ne-glect me!
2. I am your nur-ture: Do not de-stroy me!
3. I am your lodg-ing: Do not a-buse me!
4. God is our mak-er: Do not de-ny God,

Chil-dren, pro-tect me — I need your trust;
Love and en-joy me, sa-vor my fruit;
Ten-der-ly use me, sooth-ing my scars;
chal-lenge, de-fy God, threat-en this place;

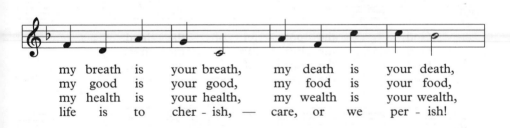

my breath is your breath, my death is your death,
my good is your good, my food is your food,
my health is your health, my wealth is your wealth,
life is to cher-ish, — care, or we per-ish!

ash-es to ash-es, dust in-to dust.
wa-ter and flow-er, branch-es and root.
shin-ing with prom-ise, set a-mong stars.
I am your moth-er, — tears on my face.

WORDS: Shirley Erena Murray
MUSIC: Per Harling

EARTH PRAYER
55.54 D

2060 God the Sculptor of the Mountains

1. God the sculp-tor of the moun-tains,
2. God the nui-sance to the Pha-raoh,
3. God the dress-er of the vine-yard,
4. God the un-ex-pect-ed in-fant,

God the mill-er of the sand,
God the cleav-er of the sea,
God the plant-er of the wheat,
God the calm, de-ter-mined youth,

God the jewel-er of the heav-ens,
God the pil-lar in the dark-ness,
God the reap-er of the har-vest,
God the ta-ble-turn-ing proph-et,

God the pot-ter of the land:
God the bea-con of the free:
God the source of all we eat:
God the re-sur-rect-ed truth:

You are womb of all cre-a-tion,
You are fount of all de-liv-'rance,
You are host at ev-ery ta-ble,
You are pres-ent ev-ery mo-ment,

we are form-less; shape us now.
we are sight-less; lead us now.
we are hun-gry; feed us now.
we are search-ing; meet us now.

WORDS: John Thornburg
MUSIC: Amanda Husberg

JENNINGS-HOUSTON
87.87.87

Creator of Mountains

1. Cre - a - tor of moun-tains, of gla - ciers and streams,
2. Cre - a - tor of peo - ples and rac - es and tribes,
3. Cre - a - ted for car - ing for all hu - man need,
4. Cre - a - tor of riv - er and for - est and snow,
5. Great God, now we come, our hearts grate - ful for days

Great Splash-er of foun-tains and Dream - er of dreams,
not bound by church stee - ples or what myth de - scribes,
we seek to be dar - ing in thought and in deed.
E - ter - nal Life - giv - er whose pres - ence we know,
when faith, like a drum-beat, keeps stead - y our praise.

we gath - er in won - der and praise for Your grace.
we cel - e - brate now our di - ver - si - ty here,
Turn us from all strife that de - means or di - vides.
Your voice is re - sound-ing in storm, wind, and wave.
In song and re - joic - ing hopes stir and a - rise,

Re - spond-ing, we pon - der our work in this place.
in pen - i - tence vow to ac - cept and not fear.
Re - form us for life that em - powers and a - bides.
Your love is a - bound-ing, em - brac - ing to save.
our spir - its now voic - ing their hymns to the skies.

WORDS: Jane Parker Huber
MUSIC: Welsh folk melody
ST. DENIO
11 11.11 11
Words © 1996 Jane Parker Huber

2062 The Lily of the Valley

1. I have found a friend in Je - sus, he's ev - ery-thing to me,
2. He all my grief has tak - en, and all my sor-rows borne;
3. He will nev - er, nev - er leave me, nor yet for - sake me here,

he's the fair - est of ten thou-sand to my soul;
in temp - ta - tion he's my strong and might - y tower;
while I live by faith and do his bless - ed will;

the Lil - y of the Val - ley, in him a - lone I see
I have all for him for - sak - en, and all my i - dols torn
a wall of fire a - bout me, I've noth-ing now to fear,

all I need to cleanse and make me ful - ly whole.
from my heart, and now he keeps me by his power.
with his man - na he my hun - gry soul shall fill.

WORDS: Charles W. Fry (Deut. 31:6, 8; Ps. 36:8; Song of Sol. 2:1; 5:10; Hab. 2:4; Rom. 1:17;
Rev. 2:17; 22:16)
MUSIC: William S. Hays; adapt. by Charles W. Fry

SALVATIONIST
Irregular

In   sor - row he's my com-fort,   in   trou-ble he's my stay,
Though   all   the world for-sake me,   and   Sa - tan tempts me sore,
Then   sweep-ing up to glo - ry,   to   see his bless - ed   face,

he   tells me ev - ery care on him to   roll.
through   Je - sus   I   shall safe - ly reach the   goal.
where   riv - ers of de - light shall ev - er   roll.

Hal - le - lu - jah!

He's the   Lil - y   of the Val - ley,   the bright and Morn-ing Star,

he's the   fair - est   of   ten thou-sand to   my   soul.

2063 You Are Worthy
(Eres Digno)

You are wor - thy, _____ God al - might - y, _____ praise and
E - res dig - no, _____ e - res dig - no, _____ e - res

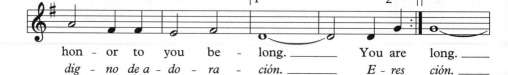

|1|2|
hon - or to you be - long. _____ You are long. _____
dig - no de a - do - ra - ción. _____ E - res ción. _____

_____ King all glo - rious, ___ all vic - to - rious, ___ praise and
— Rey glo - rio - so, _____ ma - jes - tuo - so, _____ e - res

|1|2|
hon - or are yours a - lone. _____ King all lone. _____
dig - no de a - do - ra - ción. _____ Rey glo - ción. _____

WORDS: Trad. Latin American; English trans. by Raquel Mora Martínez (Rev. 4:11)
MUSIC: Trad. Latin American

DIGNO
LM

2064 O Lord, You're Beautiful

1., 3. O Lord, you're beau - ti - ful, your face is all I seek; and
2. O Lord, you're won - der - ful, your touch is all I need; and

when your eyes are on this child, your grace a - bounds to me.
when your hand is on this child, your heal - ing I re - ceive.

WORDS: Keith Green (Ps. 27:4, 8; Luke 5:12-13; Rom. 5:15)
MUSIC: Keith Green

BEAUTIFUL
SM

More Precious than Silver 2065

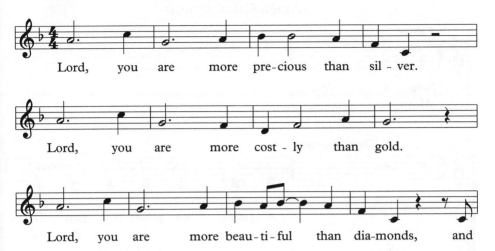

Lord, you are more pre-cious than sil - ver.

Lord, you are more cost - ly than gold.

Lord, you are more beau-ti-ful than dia-monds, and

noth-ing I de - sire com-pares with you. _____

WORDS: Lynn DeShazo (Ps. 16:2; 119:72; Prov. 3:13-15; 1 Pet. 2:7)
MUSIC: Lynn DeShazo

DESHAZO
Irregular

Praise the Name of Jesus 2066

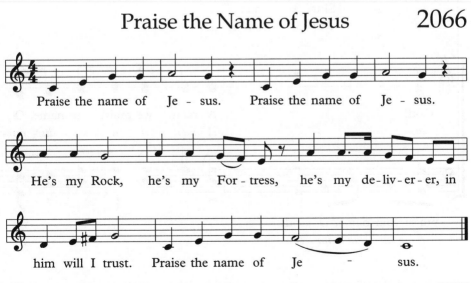

Praise the name of Je - sus. Praise the name of Je - sus.

He's my Rock, he's my For - tress, he's my de - liv - er - er, in

him will I trust. Praise the name of Je - sus.

WORDS: Roy Hicks Jr. (Ps. 18:2)
MUSIC: Roy Hicks Jr.

HICKS
Irregular

2067 Amen, We Praise Your Name, O God
(Amen Siakudumisa)

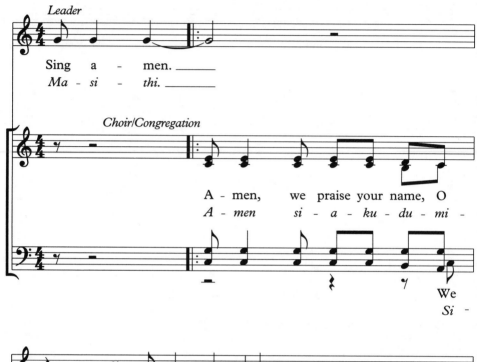

WORDS: Trad. Xhosa (South Africa); attr. to S. C. Molefe as taught by George Mxadana
MUSIC: Trad. Xhosa melody (South Africa); attr. to S. C. Molefe as taught by George Mxadana
© 1996 General Board of Global Ministries, GBGMusik

MASITHI
Irregular

Sing a - men. ____
Ma - si - thi. ____

God.
sa.

A - men, ba - wo,
A - men, ba - wo,

praise your name, O God.
a - ku - du - mi - sa.

Ba - wo, ba -
Ba - wo, ba -

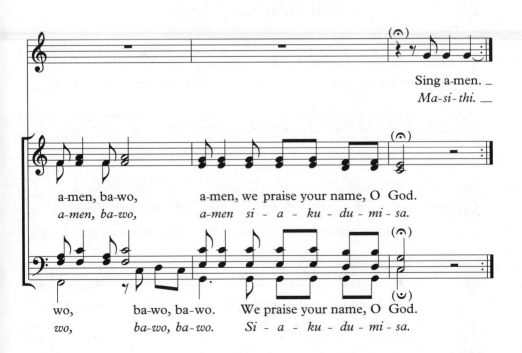

Sing a-men. _
Ma-si-thi. _

a-men, ba-wo,
a-men, ba-wo,

a-men, we praise your name, O God.
a-men si - a - ku - du - mi - sa.

wo,
wo,

ba-wo, ba-wo.
ba-wo, ba-wo.

We praise your name, O God.
Si - a - ku - du - mi - sa.

2068   I Love You, Lord

I love you, Lord, ___ and I lift my voice ___ to
wor - ship you, O my soul re - joice. Take
joy, my King, ___ in what you hear, ___ may it be a
sweet, sweet sound in your ear. ___

WORDS: Laurie Klein (Ps. 35:9)   I LOVE YOU, LORD
MUSIC: Laurie Klein   Irregular

2069   All Hail King Jesus

All hail King Je - sus! ___ All hail Em - man - u - el, ___
___ King of kings, Lord of lords, bright Morn - ing Star. ___
___ And through-out e - ter - ni - ty, I'll sing your prais - es; ___
___ and I'll reign with you through-out e - ter - ni - ty. ___

WORDS: Dave Moody (Matt. 1:23; 2 Tim. 2:12; Rev. 19:16; 22:16)   KING JESUS
MUSIC: Dave Moody   Irregular

He Is Exalted

He is ex-alt-ed, the King is ex-alt-ed on high; I will
praise him. He is ex-alt-ed, for-ev-er ex-alt-ed and I will
praise his name! __ He is the Lord, for-ev-er his truth shall
reign; heav-en and earth re-joice in his ho-ly name.
He is ex-alt-ed, the King is ex-alt-ed on high. _____

WORDS: Twila Paris (1 Chron. 29:11; Eph. 2:19-22)
MUSIC: Twila Paris

HE IS EXALTED
Irregular

© 1985 Straightway Music/Mountain Spring Music

Jesus, Name above All Names

Je - sus, name a-bove all names, beau-ti-ful
Sav - ior, glo-ri-ous Lord. Em-man-u-el, God is
with us, bless-ed Re-deem-er, liv-ing Word.

WORDS: Naida Hearn (Matt. 1:23; John 1:14; Phil. 2:9)
MUSIC: Naida Hearn

NAME ABOVE ALL NAMES
Irregular

© 1974 Scripture in Song (c/o Integrity Music, Inc.)

2072 Blessed Be Your Holy Name

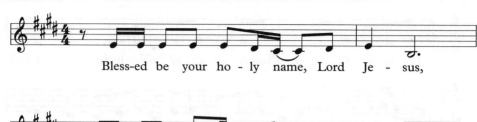

Bless-ed be your ho-ly name, Lord Je - sus,

I will nev-er cease to give you praise. You are Mes-

si - ah, De - liv - er - er, the Ho - ly One of

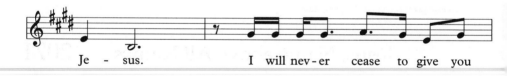

Is - ra - el. Bless-ed be your ho - ly name, Lord

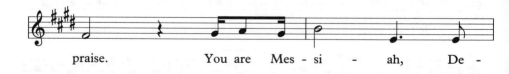

Je - sus. I will nev - er cease to give you

praise. You are Mes - si - ah, De -

Fine

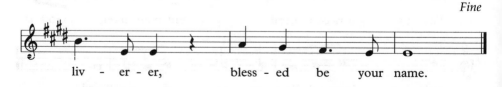

liv - er - er, bless - ed be your name.

WORDS: Eddie Espinosa
MUSIC: Eddie Espinosa

BLESSED BE YOUR HOLY NAME
Irregular with Refrain

Your name is high a - bove all oth - ers.

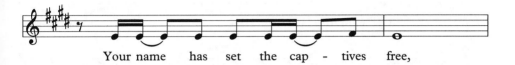

Your name has set the cap - tives free,

Your name de - liv - ers all the na - tions.

D.C. al Fine

Your name is life and breath to me. __

2073 Celebrate Love

Refrain

Cel - e - brate love, love, love. _ Cel - e - brate love, love, love. _

_ Cel - e - brate love _ so a - maz - ing. He's cre - at -

ing his won - der - ful love in you. _

1. We can cel - e - brate his love to - day.
2. We can sing a - bout his love for us.

Je - sus loves ev - ery - one. _ We can cel - e - brate new life _
Je - sus loves ev - ery - one. _ He is liv - ing here in - side _

_ to - day. Je - sus loves ev - ery - one. _)
_ of us. Je - sus loves ev - ery - one. _) Cel - e - brate

WORDS: Handt Hanson
MUSIC: Handt Hanson

CELEBRATE LOVE
Irregular with Refrain

© 1991 Changing Church Forum

2074 Shout to the Lord

Shout to the Lord, all the earth, _ let us sing

pow - er and maj - es - ty, praise _ to the King.

Stanzas in other editions.

WORDS: Darlene Zschech (Ps. 47:1; 92:4; 96:1, 6, 10; 98:7-9; Isa. 49:13)
MUSIC: Darlene Zschech

ZSCHECH
Irregular

© 1993 Darlene Zschech/Hillsongs Publishing (admin. in the U.S. and Canada by Integrity's Hosanna! Music)

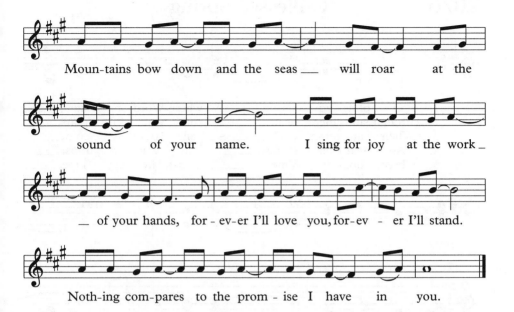

Moun-tains bow down and the seas ___ will roar at the sound of your name. I sing for joy at the work ___ of your hands, for - ev-er I'll love you, for-ev - er I'll stand.

Noth-ing com-pares to the prom - ise I have in you.

King of Kings
2075

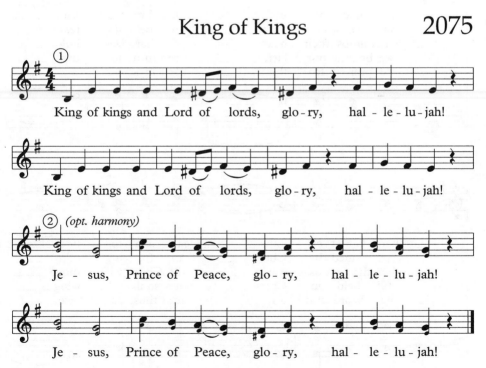

① King of kings and Lord of lords, glo-ry, hal - le - lu - jah!

King of kings and Lord of lords, glo-ry, hal - le - lu - jah!

② *(opt. harmony)*

Je - sus, Prince of Peace, glo-ry, hal - le - lu - jah!

Je - sus, Prince of Peace, glo-ry, hal - le - lu - jah!

May be sung as a canon.

WORDS: Sophie Conty and Naomi Batya (Isa. 9:6; Rev. 17:14)
MUSIC: Anon.

KING OF KINGS
Irregular

2076 O Blessed Spring

1. O bless - ed spring, _____ where Word and sign _____
2. Through sum - mer heat _____ and youth - ful years, _____
3. When au - tumn cools _____ and youth is cold, _____
4. As win - ter comes, _____ as win - ters must, _____
5. Christ, ho - ly Vine, _____ Christ, liv - ing Tree, _____

_ em - brace us in - to Christ the Vine: _____
_ un - cer - tain faith, _____ re - bel - lious tears, _____
_ when limbs their heav - y har - vest hold, _____
_ we breathe our last, _____ re - turn to dust; _____
_ be praised for this _____ blest mys - ter - y: _____

_ here Christ en - joins _____ each one to be _____
_ sus - tained by Christ's _____ in - fus - ing rain, _____
_ then through us warm, _____ the Christ will move _____
_ still held in Christ, _____ our souls take wing _____
_ that Word and wa - ter thus re - vive _____

WORDS: Susan Palo Cherwien (John 15:5; Rev. 22:14)
MUSIC: Trad. English melody; adapt. by Hal H. Hopson

GIFT OF LOVE
LM

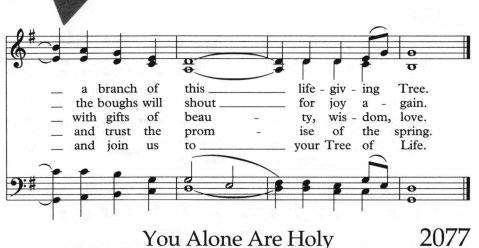

— a branch of this _____ life - giv - ing Tree.
— the boughs will shout _____ for joy a - gain.
— with gifts of beau - ty, wis - dom, love.
— and trust the prom - ise of the spring.
— and join us to _____ your Tree of Life.

You Alone Are Holy 2077
(Sólo Tú Eres Santo)

1. You a-lone are ho - ly; _____ you a-lone are wor - thy; ___
2. You a-lone are ho - ly; _____ you a-lone are wor - thy; ___
1. *Só - lo tú e - res san - to, _____ só - lo tú e - res dig - no, ___*
2. *Só - lo tú e - res san - to, _____ só - lo tú e - res dig - no, ___*

— you are filled with splen - dor ____ and with awe-some won - der. —
— you are filled with splen - dor ____ and with awe-some won - der. —
— *tú e - res her - mo - so _____ y ma - ra - vi - llo - so. ___*
— *tú e - res her - mo - so _____ y ma - ra - vi - llo - so. ___*

— For our sins you suf - fered, _ died and res - ur-rect - ed, ___
— Send your Ho - ly Spir - it; _____ may it shine up - on us. ___
— *En la cruz mo - ris - te _____ y re - su - ci - tas - te; ___*
— *De - rra - ma tu Es-pí - ri - tu _____ y que tu luz bri - lle; ___*

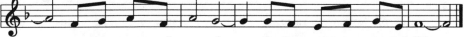

— grant-ing us sal - va - tion, _ giv-ing us e - ter-nal life. ___
— Let your won-drous glo - ry ____ with its ra-diance fill this place. _
— *tú me dis - te vi - da ____ y muy pron - to vol - ve - rás. ___*
— *que tu glo - ria lle - ne ____ aho - ra mis-mo es - te lu - gar. ___*

WORDS: St. 1 anon.; adapt. by Kenneth R. Hanna; st. 2 by Jorge Lockward;
English trans. by Raquel Mora Martínez (Rev. 4:11)
MUSIC: Anon.

QUERÉTARO
12 12.12 13

St. 2 © 1996, trans. © 2000 Abingdon Press (admin. by The Copyright Co., Nashville, TN)

2078 Alleluia

Al - le - lu - ia. Al - le - lu - ia. Al - le - lu - ia. Al - le - lu - ia. Al - le -

lu - ia. Al - le - lu - ia. Now the Lord is ris'n in - deed. _
El Se - ñor re - su - ci - tó. ____

Stanzas included in other editions.

WORDS: Trad. Honduran
MUSIC: Trad. Honduran

HONDURAS ALLELUIA
Irregular

2079 Jesus Be Praised

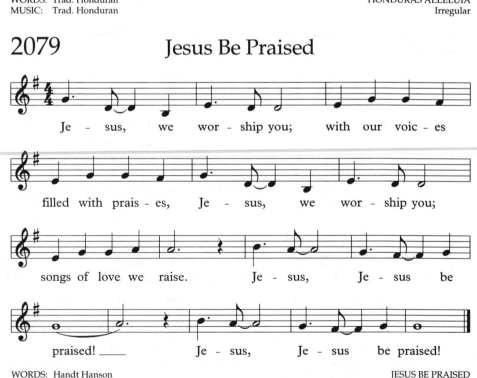

Je - sus, we wor - ship you; with our voic - es

filled with prais - es, Je - sus, we wor - ship you;

songs of love we raise. Je - sus, Je - sus be

praised! ____ Je - sus, Je - sus be praised!

WORDS: Handt Hanson
MUSIC: Handt Hanson

JESUS BE PRAISED
Irregular

All I Need Is You

2080

1. __ All I need is you, Je-sus,
2. __ All I want is you, Je-sus,
3. My on - ly hope is you, Lord, my

all I need is you. You are the source of
all I want is you. You are the source of
on - ly hope is you. You are the source of

all I need. ____ All I need is you.
all I want. ____ All I want is you.
all I need. My on - ly hope is you.

WORDS: Dan Adler
MUSIC: Dan Adler

ADLER
Irregular

© 1989 Heart of the City Music

Thank You, Jesus
(Tino Tenda, Jesu)

2081

Thank you, Je-sus, a-men! Thank you, Je-sus, a-men! Thank you,
Ti - no ten-da, Je-su! Ti - no ten-da, Je-su! Ti - no

Je - sus, a - men! Al - le - lu - ia! A - men!
ten - da, Je - su! Ha - le - lu - jah! A - men!

WORDS: Trad. Shona; trans. by Patrick Matsikenyiri (Ps. 118:21; Rev. 11:17; 19:4)
MUSIC: African folk song; transcribed and arr. by Patrick Matsikenyiri

TINO TENDA
Irregular

© 1996 General Board of Global Ministries, GBGMusik

2082　Woke Up This Morning

Leader
1. Oh, I woke up this morn-ing with my mind, and it was stayed, woke up this morn-ing with my

All
Stayed on Je - sus,

mind, and it was stayed,

Stayed on Je - sus,

WORDS: African American spiritual
MUSIC: African American spiritual; arr. by J. Jefferson Cleveland and Verolga Nix

WOKE UP THIS MORNING
Irregular

Arr. © 1981 Abingdon Press (admin. by The Copyright Co., Nashville, TN)

woke up this morn - ing with my mind, and it was stayed, Hal-le - lu, Hal-le - lu, Hal-le - lu, Hal-le - lu - jah.

Stayed on Je - sus, Hal-le - lu, Hal-le - lu, Hal-le - lu - jah.

2. Oh, you can't hate your neighbor in your mind, if you keep it stayed, ...
3. Makes you love everybody with your mind, when you keep it stayed, ...
4. Oh, the devil can't catch you in your mind, if you keep it stayed, ...
5. Oh, yes, Jesus is the captain in your mind, when you keep it stayed, ...

2083   My Song Is Love Unknown

1. My song is love un-known, my Sav-ior's love to me, love to the love-less shown, that they might love-ly be. O who am I, that for my sake my God should take frail

2. God left the rich-est throne sal-va-tion to be-stow; but Christ as flesh and bone the world re-fused to know. But, O my Friend, my Friend in-deed, who at my need did

3. Some-times they threw down palms and sweet-est prais-es sang. Ho-san-nas and glad psalms through streets and mar-kets rang. Then "Cru-ci-fy!" is all their breath, for blood and death they

4. What has my Sov-ereign done? What makes this rage and spite? Christ gave new strength to run, re-stored the gift of sight. Sweet in-ju-ries! Yet they them-selves dis-please, and

5. I sing my plain be-lief, one song my heart out-pours: nev-er was pain nor grief, nev-er was love like yours. This is my Friend, in whose sweet praise I all my days could

WORDS: Samuel Crossman (2 Cor. 5:15-19; Heb. 5:7-10)
MUSIC: John D. Edwards

RHOSYMEDRE
66.66.888

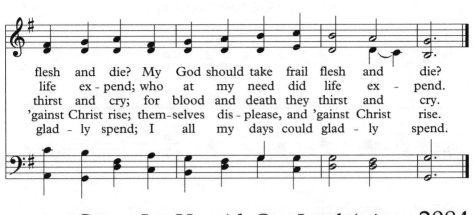

flesh and die? My God should take frail flesh and die?
life ex-pend; who at my need did life ex-pend.
thirst and cry; for blood and death they thirst and cry.
'gainst Christ rise; them-selves dis-please, and 'gainst Christ rise.
glad-ly spend; I all my days could glad-ly spend.

Come, Let Us with Our Lord Arise 2084

1. Come, let us with our Lord a-rise, our
2. This is the day the Lord has made, that
3. Then let us ren-der him his own, with

Lord, who made both earth and skies: who died to save the
all may see his love dis-played, may feel his res-ur-
sol-emn prayer ap-proach his throne, with meek-ness hear the

world he made, and rose tri-um-phant from the dead;
rec-tion's power, and rise a-gain, to fall no more,
gos-pel word, with thanks his dy-ing love re-cord,

he rose, the Prince of life and peace,
in per-fect righ-teous-ness re-newed,
our joy-ful hearts and voic-es raise,

and stamped the day for-ev-er his.
and filled with all the life of God.
and fill his courts with songs of praise.

WORDS: Charles Wesley (Ps. 118:24; 1 Cor. 6:14; Heb. 4:16)
MUSIC: Trad. English melody

SUSSEX CAROL
88.88.88

2085 He Came Down

He came down that we may have { love; peace; joy; } he
came down that we may have { love; peace; joy; } he came down that we may
Leader: Why did he come?
have { love, peace, joy; } Hal-le - lu - jah for - ev - er - more.

WORDS: Trad. Cameroon
MUSIC: Trad. Cameroon; trans. and arr. by John Bell

HE CAME DOWN
Irregular

2086 Open Our Eyes

O - pen our eyes, Lord, _____ we want to see Je -

WORDS: Bob Cull (John 12:21; Eph. 1:17-18)
MUSIC: Bob Cull

OPEN OUR EYES
Irregular

sus, _____ to reach out and touch him, _____ and
say that we love him. _____ O - pen our ears, Lord, _
_ and help us to lis - ten. _____ O - pen our
eyes, Lord, _____ we want to see Je - sus. _____

We Will Glorify the King of Kings   2087

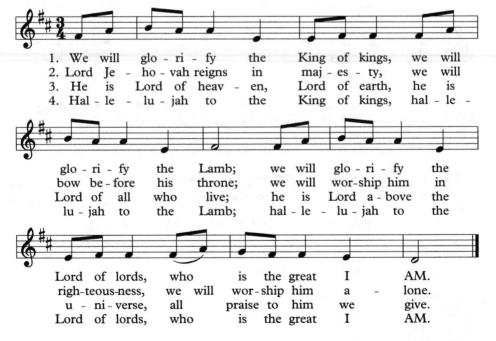

1. We will glo - ri - fy the King of kings, we will
2. Lord Je - ho - vah reigns in maj - es - ty, we will
3. He is Lord of heav - en, Lord of earth, he is
4. Hal - le - lu - jah to the King of kings, hal - le -

glo - ri - fy the Lamb; we will glo - ri - fy the
bow be - fore his throne; we will wor - ship him in
Lord of all who live; he is Lord a - bove the
lu - jah to the Lamb; hal - le - lu - jah to the

Lord of lords, who is the great I AM.
righ - teous - ness, we will wor - ship him a - lone.
u - ni - verse, all praise to him we give.
Lord of lords, who is the great I AM.

WORDS: Twila Paris (Ps. 93:1; Rev. 17:14)
MUSIC: Twila Paris

WE WILL GLORIFY
97.96

2088 Lord, I Lift Your Name on High

Lord, I lift your name on high;

Lord, I love to sing your prais - es.

I'm so glad you're in my life;

I'm so glad you came to save us.

You came from heav - en to earth _ to show the way, _

_ from the earth _____ to the cross _ my debt to pay; _

_ from the cross to the grave, _ from the grave to the sky; _

_ Lord, I lift your name on high.

WORDS: Rick Founds (1 Cor. 15:3-4)
MUSIC: Rick Founds

LIFT YOUR NAME ON HIGH
Irregular

IN PRAISE OF CHRIST, *see further:*

2026   Halle, Halle, Halleluja
2272   Holy Ground
2032   My Life Is in You, Lord
2009   O God Beyond All Praising
2258   Sing Alleluia to the Lord

Wild and Lone the Prophet's Voice 2089

1. Wild and lone the proph-et's voice ech - oes
2. "Bear the fruit re - pen - tance sows: lives of
3. With such preach - ing stark and bold John pro -

through the des - ert still, call - ing us to make a
jus - tice, truth, and love. Trust no oth - er claim than
claimed sal - va - tion near, and his time - less warn - ings

choice, bid-ding us to do God's will: "Turn from
those; set your heart on things a - bove. Soon the
hold words of hope to all who hear. So we

sin and be bap - tized; cleanse your heart and mind and
Lord will come in power, burn - ing clean the thresh-ing
dare to jour-ney on, led by faith through ways un -

soul. Quit - ting all the sin you
floor: then will flames the chaff de -
trod, till we come at last like

prized, yield your life to God's con - trol.
vour; wheat a - lone shall fill God's store."
John— to be - hold the Lamb of God.

WORDS: Carl P. Daw Jr. (Matt. 3; Mark 1:1-11; Luke 3:1-22; John 1:19-37)
MUSIC: David Ashley White

LA GRANGE
77.77 D

Words © 1989 Hope Publishing Co.; music © 1996 Selah Publishing Co.

2090   Advent Song

1. Light the Ad - vent can - dle, one: Now the
2. Light the Ad - vent can - dle, two: Think of
3. Light the Ad - vent can - dle, three: Think of
4. Light the Ad - vent can - dle, four: Think of
5. Light the Christ - mas can - dles, now: Sing of

wait - ing has be - gun; we have start - ed
hum - ble shep - herds, who filled with won - der
heaven - ly har - mo - ny; an - gels sing - ing
joy for - ev - er - more; Christ Child in a
don - key, sheep, and cow; birth - day can - dles

on our way, time to think of Christ - mas day.
at the sight of the child of Christ - mas night.
"Peace on earth" at the bless - ed Sav - ior's birth.
sta - ble born, gift of love that Christ - mas morn.
for the King, let the al - le - lu - ias ring.

Refrain

Can - dle, can - dle, burn - ing bright, shin - ing

in the cold win - ter night; can - dle, can - dle,

burn - ing bright, fill our hearts with Christ - mas light.

WORDS: Mary Lu Walker (Luke 2:1-20)   ADVENT CANDLE SONG
MUSIC: Mary Lu Walker   77.77 with Refrain

© 1998 Mary Lu Walker

The King of Glory Comes 2091

Refrain

The King of glo - ry comes, the na - tion re - joic - es.

Fine

O - pen the gates be - fore him, lift up your voic - es.

1. Who is the King of glo - ry; how shall we call him?
2. In all of Gal - i - lee, in cit - y or vil - lage,
3. Sing then of Da - vid's son, our Sav - ior and broth - er;

D.C.

He is Em - man - u - el, the prom - ised of a - ges.
he goes a - mong his peo - ple cur - ing their ill - ness.
in all of Gal - i - lee was nev - er an - oth - er.

WORDS: Rev. Willard F. Jabusch (Ps. 24:7-10; Matt. 1:23)   KING OF GLORY
MUSIC: Trad. Israeli folk song   12 12 with Refrain

Words © 1966, 1982 Willard F. Jabusch (admin. by OCP Publications)

like a child 2092

1. like a child love would send to re - veal and to mend, like a
2. like a child we will meet, rag - ged clothes, dirt - y feet, like a
3. like a child born to pray and to show us the way, like a

child and a friend, Je - sus comes. like a child we may find claim-ing
child on the street, Je - sus comes. like a child we once knew com - ing
child here to stay, Je - sus comes. like a child we re - ceive all that

heart, soul, and mind, like a child strong and kind, Je - sus comes.
back in - to view, like a child born a - new, Je - sus comes.
love can con - ceive, like a child we be - lieve, Je - sus comes.

WORDS: Daniel Charles Damon (Matt. 19:13-15; Mark 10:13-16; Luke 18:15-17)   LIKE A CHILD
MUSIC: Daniel Charles Damon   66.63 D

© 1993 Hope Publishing Co.

2093 O Laughing Light

1. O Laugh-ing Light, O first - born of cre-
2. Day's light is frag - ile. Your light is e -
3. Light of the world, O Je - sus, you are

a - tion, ra - diance of glo - ry, light from light be -
ter - nal. We look to you, our light with - in the
wor - thy! Giv - er of Life and Child of God, we

got - ten, God self - re - veal - ing, ho - ly,
shad - ow. We sing to you, __ Cre - a - tor,
praise you. Hear as the u - ni - verse now pro -

bright and bless - ed, You shine up - on us.
Christ and Spir - it; You shine be - fore us.
claims your glo - ry! You shine a - mong us.

WORDS: Sylvia G. Dunstan
MUSIC: Rouen church melody
Words © 1991 GIA Publications, Inc.

ISTE CONFESSOR
11 11.11 5

2094 Carol of the Epiphany

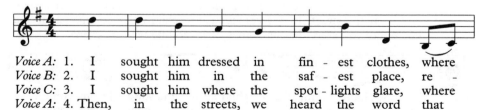

Voice A: 1. I sought him dressed in fin - est clothes, where
Voice B: 2. I sought him in the saf - est place, re -
Voice C: 3. I sought him where the spot - lights glare, where
Voice A: 4. Then, in the streets, we heard the word that
All: 5. And so, dis - tinct from all we'd planned, a -

WORDS: John Bell (Matt. 2:1-12)
MUSIC: John Bell
© 1992 WGRG The Iona Community (Scotland). Used by permission of GIA Publications, Inc.

FIRST HAND
LM

mon - ey talks and stat - us grows; but power and wealth he
mote from crime or cheap dis - grace; but safe - ty nev - er
crowds col - lect and crit - ics stare; but no one knew his
seemed, for all the world, ab - surd: That those who could no
mong the poor - est of the land, we did what few might

nev - er chose: It seemed he lived in pov - er - ty.
knew his face: It seemed he lived in jeop - ar - dy.
pres - ence there: It seemed he lived in ob - scu - ri - ty.
gifts af - ford were en - ter - tain - ing Christ the Lord.
un - der - stand: We touched God in a ba - by's hand.

Star-Child

2095

1. Star - Child, earth - Child, go - be - tween of God,
2. Street child, beat child, no place left to go,
3. Grown child, old child, mem - ory full of years,
4. Spared child, spoiled child, hav - ing, want - ing more,
5. Hope - for - peace Child, God's stu - pend - ous sign,

love Child, Christ Child, heav - en's light - ning rod,
hurt child, used child, no one wants to know,
sad child, lost child, sto - ry told in tears,
wise child, faith child, know - ing joy in store,
down - to - earth Child, Star of stars that shine,

Refrain

This year, this year, let the day ar - rive when

Christ - mas comes for ev - ery - one, ev - ery - one a - live!

WORDS: Shirley Erena Murray (Matt. 2:1-12)
MUSIC: Carlton R. Young

STAR CHILD
45.45 with Refrain

© 1994 Hope Publishing Co.

2096 Rise Up, Shepherd, and Follow

(There's a Star in the East)

Leader

1. There's a star in the East on Christ-mas morn;
2. If you take good heed to the an-gel's words;

it will lead to the place where the
you'll for-get your flocks, you'll for-

All

rise up, shep-herd, and fol-low;

Christ was born;
get your herds;

rise up, shep-herd, and fol-low.

Refrain

Fol-low, fol-low, rise up, shep-herd, and fol-low,

WORDS: African American spiritual (Matt. 2:1-12; Luke 2:8-20)
MUSIC: African American spiritual

RISE UP, SHEPHERD
Irregular with Refrain

fol-low the star of Beth-le-hem. Rise up, shep-herd, and fol-low.

One Holy Night in Bethlehem 2097

1. One ho-ly night in Beth-le-hem the
2. Their mu-sic ech-oed through the town in -
3. As Jo-seph touched the lamb's soft wool and
4. Be still, and you will hear to-night these

air was filled with song. An-gel-ic voic-es
to the sta-ble stall, where Mar-y sang a
fed the don-key hay, he whis-tled his own
mel-o-dies of old. Then join your voice in

sang on high and shep-herds piped a-long:
lul-la-by and rocked her ba-by small:
hap-py tune and thanked God for this day:
har-mo-ny un-til the tale is told:

Refrain

Sing glo-ry, glo-ry, glo-ri-a! God's love is giv-en birth! Be

not a-fraid! Sing glo-ri-a, and peace to all the earth!

WORDS: Mary Nelson Keithahn (Luke 2:8-20)
MUSIC: John D. Horman

WHISTLER'S TUNE
CM with Refrain

© 1998 Abingdon Press (admin. by The Copyright Co., Nashville, TN)

2098   The Baby in a Manger Stall

1. The baby in a manger stall is God In-car-nate for us all, as God, true God, the only One, is born on earth as Mar-y's Son.

2. We can-not keep the Sav-ior there, for Christ is meant for ev-ery-where, not just for shep-herds' watch-ful eyes, nor for a wise man's val-ued prize.

3. As God's own per-son here on earth, Christ came to show us hu-man worth, so Je-sus can-not stay a child, de-pen-dent, gen-tle, meek, and mild.

4. The Car-pen-ter of Gal-i-lee must leave his shop and home, as he takes up the mis-sion and the pain of life and death and life a-gain!

5. So glad-ly let us sing and pray since Christ is born for us each day, and Christ is risen with God to reign. Let earth re-peat the glad re-frain.

6. Glo-ry to God in depth and height! Al-le-lu-ia! from dawn through night! All space and time in Christ re-joice, in praise to God, a sin-gle voice!

WORDS: Jane Parker Huber (Matt. 1:18-2:12; Luke 2:1-20)
MUSIC: Thomas Tallis

TALLIS' CANON
LM

Joseph Dearest, Joseph Mine

2099

1. Jo - seph dear - est, Jo - seph mine, help me cra - dle the
2. Glad - ly, dear one, la - dy mine, help I cra - dle this
3. All shall come and bow the knee; wise and hap - py their

child di - vine; God re - ward thee and all that's thine in
child of thine; God's own light on us both shall shine in
souls shall be, lov - ing such a di - vin - i - ty, as

par - a - dise, so prays the moth - er Ma - ry.
par - a - dise, as prays the moth - er Ma - ry.
all may see in Je - sus, Son of Ma - ry.

Refrain

He came a - mong us at Christ - mas - time, at
Christ - mas - time, in Beth - le - hem; let us bring him from
far and wide Love's di - a - dem: Je - sus, Je - sus,
lo, he comes, and loves, and saves, and frees us!

WORDS: Trad. German (Luke 2:1-20)
MUSIC: Trad. German

JOSEPH LIEBER, JOSEPH MEIN
78.847 with Refrain

2100 Thou Didst Leave Thy Throne

1. Thou didst leave thy throne and thy king - ly crown,
2. Heav - en's arch - es rang when the an - gels sang,
3. The fox - es found rest, and the birds their nest
4. Thou camest, O Lord, with the liv - ing Word
5. When heav'ns arch - es shall ring and its choir shall sing

when thou cam - est to earth for me; but in
pro - claim - ing thy roy - al de - gree; but in
in the shade of the for - est tree; but thy
that should set thy peo - ple free; but with
at thy com - ing to vic - to - ry, let thy

Beth - le - hem's home there was found no room
low - ly birth didst thou come to earth,
couch was the sod, O thou Son of God,
mock - ing scorn, and with crown of thorn,
voice call me home, say - ing "Yet there is room,

WORDS: Timothy R. Matthews (Phil. 2:5-11)
MUSIC: Emily E. S. Elliott

MARGARET
Irregular

for thy ho - ly na - tiv - i - ty.
and in great hu - mil - i - ty.
in the des - erts of Gal - i - lee.
they bore thee to Cal - va - ry.
there is room at my side for thee!"

O come to my heart, Lord Je - sus,
O come to my heart, Lord Je - sus,
O come to my heart, Lord Je - sus,
O come to my heart, Lord Je - sus,
And my heart shall re - joice, Lord Je - sus,

there is room in my heart for thee.
there is room in my heart for thee.
there is room in my heart for thee.
there is room in my heart for thee.
when thou com - est and callest for me.

2101 Two Fishermen

1. Two fish - er - men, who lived a - long the
2. And as he walked a - long the shore 'twas
3. O Si - mon Pe - ter, An - drew, James, and
4. And you, good Chris - tians, one and all who'd

Sea of Gal - i - lee, stood by the shore to
James and John he'd find, and these two sons of
John be - lov - ed one, you heard Christ's call to
fol - low Je - sus' way, come leave be - hind what

cast their nets in - to an age - less sea. Now
Zeb - e - dee would leave their boats be - hind. Their
speak good news re - vealed to God's own Son. Su -
keeps you bound to trap - pings of our day, and

Je - sus watched them from a - far, then called them each by
work and all they held so dear they left be - side their
san - na, Ma - ry, Mag - da - lene who trav - eled with your
lis - ten as he calls your name to come and fol - low

name. It changed their lives, these sim - ple men; they'd
nets. Their names they'd heard as Je - sus called; they
Lord, you min - is - tered to him with joy for
near; for still he speaks in var - ied ways to

Refrain

nev - er be the same.
came with-out re - gret.
he is God a - dored.   "Leave all things you have and
those his call will hear.

WORDS: Suzanne Toolan (Matt. 4:18-22; Mark 1:16-20; Luke 5:1-11; 8:1-3)
MUSIC: Suzanne Toolan

LEAVE ALL THINGS BEHIND
CMD with Refrain

Words © 1986, music © 1970 GIA Publications, Inc.

come and fol - low me, and come and fol - low me."

You, Lord, Are Both Lamb and Shepherd 2102

1. You, Lord, are both Lamb and Shep-herd. You, Lord are both
2. Clothed in light up - on the moun-tain, stripped of might up -
3. You, who walk each day be-side us, sit in pow - er
4. Wor - thy is our earth - ly Je - sus! Wor - thy is our

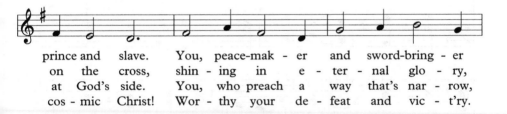

prince and slave. You, peace-mak - er and sword-bring - er
on the cross, shin - ing in e - ter - nal glo - ry,
at God's side. You, who preach a way that's nar - row,
cos - mic Christ! Wor - thy your de - feat and vic - t'ry.

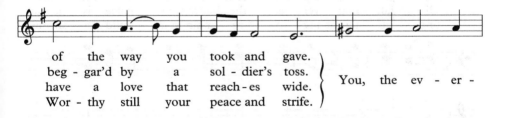

of the way you took and gave. ⎫
beg - gar'd by a sol - dier's toss. ⎬ You, the ev - er -
have a love that reach - es wide. ⎬
Wor - thy still your peace and strife. ⎭

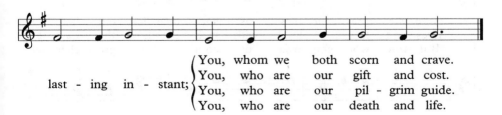

⎧ You, whom we both scorn and crave.
last - ing in - stant; ⎪ You, who are our gift and cost.
⎨ You, who are our pil - grim guide.
⎩ You, who are our death and life.

WORDS: Sylvia G. Dunstan WESTMINSTER ABBEY
MUSIC: Adapt. from an anthem by Henry Purcell 87.87.87
Words © 1991 GIA Publications, Inc.

THE GRACE OF JESUS CHRIST

2103 We Have Come at Christ's Own Bidding

1. We have come at Christ's own bid - ding to this
2. Light breaks through our clouds and shad - ows, splen - dor
3. Strength - ened by this glimpse of glo - ry, fear - ful

high and ho - ly place, where we wait with
bathes the flesh - joined Word, Mo - ses and E -
lest our faith de - cline, we, like Pe - ter,

hope and long - ing for some to - ken of God's grace.
li - jah mar - vel as the heaven - ly voice is heard.
find it tempt - ing to re - main and build a shrine.

Here we pray for new as - sur - ance that our faith is
Eyes and hearts be - hold with won - der how the Law and
But true wor - ship gives us cour - age to pro - claim what

WORDS: Carl P. Daw Jr. (Matt. 17:1-8; Mark 9:2-8; Luke 9:28-36)
MUSIC: Rowland H. Prichard; arr. by Ralph Vaughan Williams
Words © 1988 Hope Publishing Co.

HYFRYDOL
87.87D

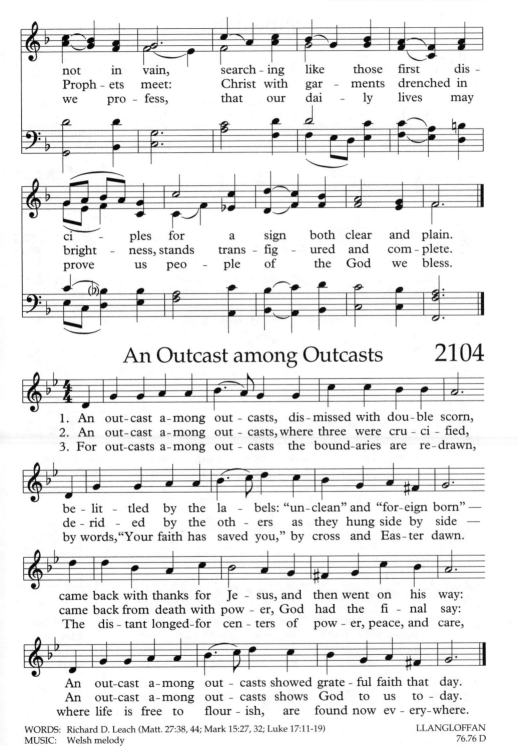

not in vain, search-ing like those first dis-
Proph-ets meet: Christ with gar - ments drenched in
we pro-fess, that our dai - ly lives may

ci - ples for a sign both clear and plain.
bright - ness, stands trans - fig - ured and com - plete.
prove us peo - ple of the God we bless.

An Outcast among Outcasts   2104

1. An out-cast a-mong out - casts, dis-missed with dou-ble scorn,
2. An out-cast a-mong out - casts, where three were cru - ci - fied,
3. For out-casts a-mong out - casts the bound-aries are re-drawn,

be - lit - tled by the la - bels: "un-clean" and "for-eign born" —
de - rid - ed by the oth - ers as they hung side by side —
by words, "Your faith has saved you," by cross and Eas-ter dawn.

came back with thanks for Je - sus, and then went on his way:
came back from death with pow - er, God had the fi - nal say:
The dis - tant longed-for cen - ters of pow - er, peace, and care,

An out-cast a-mong out - casts showed grate - ful faith that day.
An out-cast a-mong out - casts shows God to us to - day.
where life is free to flour - ish, are found now ev - ery-where.

WORDS: Richard D. Leach (Matt. 27:38, 44; Mark 15:27, 32; Luke 17:11-19)   LLANGLOFFAN
MUSIC: Welsh melody   76.76 D

2105 Jesus, Tempted in the Desert

1. Je - sus, tempt - ed in the des - ert,
2. Je - sus, tempt - ed at the tem - ple,
3. Je - sus, tempt - ed on the moun - tain
4. When we face temp - ta - tion's pow - er,

lone - ly, hun - gry, filled with dread: "Use your power," the
high a - bove its an - cient wall: "Throw your - self from
by the lure of vast do - main: "Fall be - fore me!
lone - ly, strug - gling, filled with dread, Christ, who knew the

tempt - er tells him; "Turn these bar - ren
loft - y tur - ret; an - gels wait to
Be my ser - vant! Glo - ry,
tempt - er's ho - ur, come and be our

rocks to bread!" "Not a - lone by bread," he an - swers,
break your fall!" Je - sus shuns such emp - ty mar - vels,
sure to gain!" Je - sus sees the dazz - ling vi - sion,
liv - ing bread. By your grace, pro - tect, pre - serve us

WORDS: Herman G. Stuempfle Jr. (Matt. 4:1-11; Luke 4:1-13)
MUSIC: Thomas J. Williams

EBENEZER
87.87 D

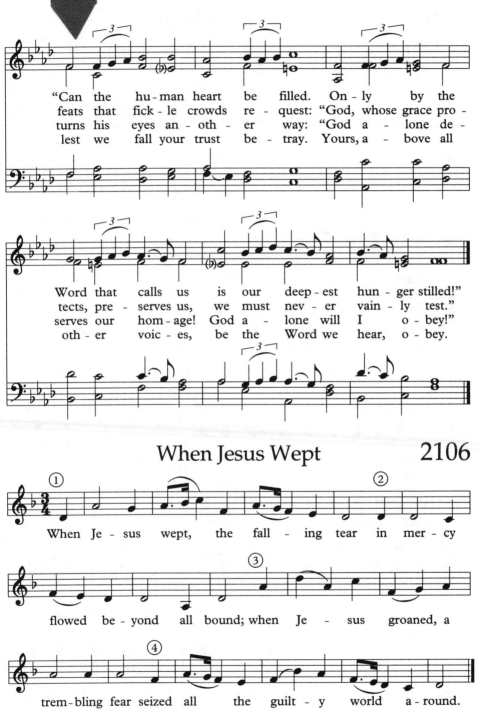

"Can the hu-man heart be filled. On-ly by the
feats that fick-le crowds re - quest: "God, whose grace pro-
turns his eyes an-oth-er way: "God a - lone de-
lest we fall your trust be - tray. Yours, a - bove all

Word that calls us is our deep-est hun - ger stilled!"
tects, pre - serves us, we must nev - er vain - ly test."
serves our hom-age! God a - lone will I o - bey!"
oth - er voic-es, be the Word we hear, o - bey.

When Jesus Wept 2106

When Je - sus wept, the fall - ing tear in mer - cy

flowed be - yond all bound; when Je - sus groaned, a

trem-bling fear seized all the guilt-y world a-round.

May be sung as a canon.

WORDS: William Billings (John 11:35)
MUSIC: William Billings

WHEN JESUS WEPT
LM

2107 Wade in the Water

WORDS: African American spiritual (John 5:2-9)   WADE IN THE WATER
MUSIC: African American spiritual; arr. by Carl Haywood   Irregular with Refrain

Arr. © 1992 Carl Haywood

CHRIST'S LIFE AND TEACHING, see further:

2278   The Lord's Prayer

O How He Loves You and Me 2108

1. O how he loves you and me! O how he
   loves you and me! He gave his life. What
   more could he give? O how he loves you; O how he
   loves me; O how he loves you and me!

2. Je - sus to Cal - v'ry did go; his love for
   sin - ners to show. What he did there brought
   hope from de - spair. O how he loves you; O how he
   loves me; O how he loves you and me!

WORDS: Kurt Kaiser (1 John 3:1)
MUSIC: Kurt Kaiser

PATRICIA
Irregular

2109 Hosanna! Hosanna!

1. Je-sus rode in-to Je-ru-sa-lem.
2. Ev-ery-bod-y brought their hopes and dreams.

Ho-

All the peo-ple sang their
Life just is-n't al-ways

san-na! Ho-san-na!

praise to him.
what it seems.

Ho-san-na! Ho-san-na!

Came to town up-on a don-key's back;
Need some-bod-y who can help us be

Ho-san-na! Ho-

seemed so low-ly but he's Lord in fact.
lib-er-at-ed from cap-tiv-i-ty.

san-na! Ho-

WORDS: Cathy Townley (Matt. 21:6-16; Mark 11:7-10; Luke 19:35-38)
MUSIC: Cathy Townley

HOSANNA! HOSANNA!
Irregular with Refrain

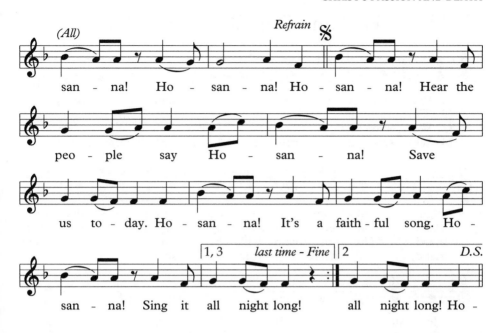

(All)

Refrain

san - na! Ho - san - na! Ho - san - na! Hear the
peo - ple say Ho - san - na! Save
us to - day. Ho - san - na! It's a faith - ful song. Ho -

1, 3   *last time - Fine*   2   *D.S.*

san - na! Sing it all night long!   all night long! Ho -

Kyrie   2110

♩ = 70

Ky-ri - e e - le - i - son,   Chris-te e - le - i - son.

Ky - ri - e e - le - i - son.   God, have mer - cy,

Christ, have mer - cy,   grant us peace.

WORDS: Ancient Greek
MUSIC: Chip Andrus   Irregular
Music © 2002 Chip Andrus

2111   We Sang Our Glad Hosannas

1. We sang our glad ho - san - nas and waved our branch - es
(2. We) heard an an - gry Je - sus in Tem - ple courts de -
(3. We) served him at the ta - ble with wine, un - leav-ened
(4. We) saw a suf-fering Je - sus a - lone, with - out a

high, but some were si - lent, frown - ing, as
clare, "Be gone, you mon - ey chang - ers! This
bread. "The one who will be - tray me now
friend, and heard the voic - es shout - ing a -

Je - sus rode on by. They sought a roy - al
is a house of prayer." Though man - y came for
eats with me," he said. His friends would not be -
buse un - til the end. We wept as we stood

Sav - ior, but did not un - der-stand a king could rule by
heal - ing and stayed to hear his word, still oth - ers, hos - tile,
lieve him, but one by one that night, as sol - diers came to
watch-ing Love's light grow dim and die, and cried, "Why did this

1-3

lov - ing in - stead of by com - mand. 2. We
plot - ted and thus his death as - sured. 3. We
take him, they scur - ried out of sight. 4. We
hap - pen? God, tell us, tell us

4

why!" *5. We bu - ried him, not know - ing that

*St. 5 for Easter Sunday. Sts. 1-4 for Palm/Passion Sunday or Holy Week

WORDS: Mary Nelson Keithahn (Matt. 21:1-17; 27:27-31, 55-56; Mark 11:15-19; 14:17-21, 43-50;   HOLY WEEK
        John 19:38-42; 20:1-18)   76.76 D
MUSIC: John D. Horman

© 1998 Abingdon Press (admin. by The Copyright Co., Nashville, TN)

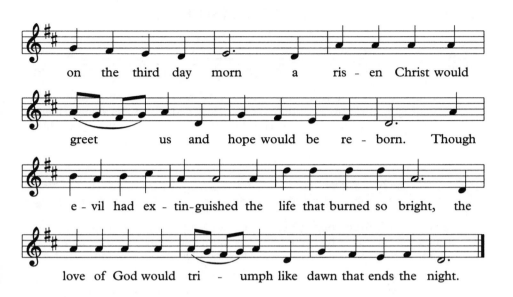

on the third day morn a - ris - en Christ would
greet us and hope would be re - born. Though
e - vil had ex - tin-guished the life that burned so bright, the
love of God would tri - umph like dawn that ends the night.

Must Jesus Bear the Cross Alone   2112

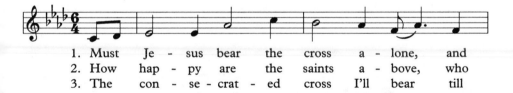

1. Must Je - sus bear the cross a - lone, and
2. How hap - py are the saints a - bove, who
3. The con - se - crat - ed cross I'll bear till

all the world go free? No, there's a cross for
once went sor - rowing here! But now they taste un -
death shall set me free; And then go home my

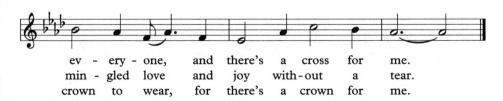

ev - ery - one, and there's a cross for me.
min - gled love and joy with-out a tear.
crown to wear, for there's a crown for me.

WORDS: Thomas Shepherd and others   MAITLAND
MUSIC: George N. Allen   CM

2113

Lamb of God

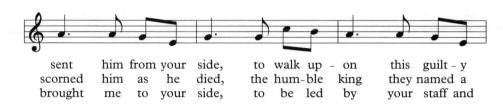

1. Your on - ly Son,   no sin to hide,   but you have
2. Your gift of love,   they cru - ci - fied,   they laughed and
3. I was so lost,   I should have died,   but you have

sent   him from your side,   to walk up - on   this guilt - y
scorned   him as he died,   the hum - ble king   they named a
brought   me to your side,   to be led by   your staff and

1

2, 3

sod,   and to be - come the Lamb of   God.   God.
fraud   and sac - ri - ficed the Lamb of   God.
rod,   and to be called a lamb of   God.

Refrain

O Lamb of God,   sweet Lamb of God,   I love the

ho - ly Lamb of God!   O wash me in   his pre - cious

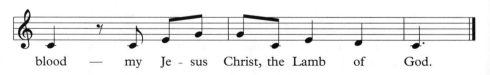

blood — my Je - sus Christ, the Lamb of God.

WORDS: Twila Paris (Ps. 23:1, 4-5; Matt. 27:37-44; Mark 15:26-32; Luke 23:35-38)   SWEET LAMB OF GOD
MUSIC: Twila Paris   Irregular with Refrain

At the Font We Start Our Journey 2114

1. At the font we start our jour - ney, in the Eas - ter
2. At the pul - pit we are fash - ioned by the Eas - ter
3. At the al - tar we are nour - ished with the Eas - ter
4. At the door we are com - mis - sioned, now the Eas - ter

faith bap - tized; doubts and fears no long - er blind us,
tale re - told in - to wit - nes - ses and proph-ets,
gift of bread; in our break-ing it to piec - es
vic-tory's won, to re - store a world di - vid - ed

by the light of Christ sur - prised. Al - le - lu - ia!
by the power of Christ made bold. Al - le - lu - ia!
see the love of Christ out - spread. Al - le - lu - ia!
to the peace of Christ as one. Al - le - lu - ia!

Al - le - lu - ia! Hope held out and re - al - ized.
Al - le - lu - ia! Faith pro - claimed, yet still un - told.
Al - le - lu - ia! Life em - braced, yet free - ly shed.
Al - le - lu - ia! Eas - ter's work must still be done.

WORDS: Jeffery Rowthorn (Acts 10:36-43; Col. 3:15)   LAUDA ANIMA
MUSIC: John Goss   87.87.87

2115 Christ Has Risen

1. Christ has ris - en while earth slum - bers,
Christ has ris - en where hope died, as he said and
as he prom - ised, as we doubt - ed
and de - nied. Let the moon em - brace the bless - ing;

2. Christ has ris - en for the peo - ple
whom he died to love and save; Christ has ris - en
for the wom - en bring - ing flowers to
grace his grave. Christ has ris - en for dis - ci - ples

3. Christ has ris - en to com - pan - ion
for - mer friends who fear the night, sens - ing loss and
lim - i - ta - tion where their faith had
once burned bright. They be - moan what is no long - er,

4. Christ has ris - en and for - ev - er
lives to chal - lenge and to change all whose lives are
messed or man - gled, all who find re -
li - gion strange. Christ is ris - en, Christ is pres - ent

WORDS: John Bell (Matt. 28; Mark 16; Luke 24; John 20–21; 1 Cor. 15:3-8)
MUSIC: William Moore

HOLY MANNA
87.87 D

let the sun sus-tain the cheer; let the world con -
hud-dled in an up-stairs room. He whose word in -
they ex-pect no hope-ful sign till Christ ends their
mak-ing us what he has been — ev-i-dence of

firm the ru-mor: Christ is ris-en, God is here!
spired cre-a-tion can't be si-lenced by the tomb.
con-ver-sa-tion, break-ing bread and shar-ing wine.
trans-for-ma-tion in which God is known and seen.

Christ the Lord Is Risen 2116

1. Christ the Lord is risen! Christ the Lord is risen! Ye - su.

Christ the Lord is risen! Christ the Lord is risen! Ye - su.

2. He has conquered death ...
3. Sin has done its worst ...
4. He is King of kings ...
5. He is Lord of lords ...

6. All the world is his ...
7. Come and worship him ...
8. Christ our Lord is risen! ...
9. Hallelujah! ...

WORDS: Tom Colvin (1 Cor. 15:20-22, 26-28, 54-57; Rev. 17:14)   GARU
MUSIC: Ghanian folk song; adapt. by Tom Colvin; arr. by Kevin R. Hackett   552.552

2117
Spirit of God

1. Spir-it of God, bright Wind, breath that bids life be - gin, blow as you al - ways do; cre - ate us a - new. _____ Give us the breath to sing, lift - ed on soar - ing wing, held in your hands, _____ borne on your wings. __
2. Spir-it of God, bright Dove, grant us your peace and love, heal-ing up - on your wings for all liv - ing things. _____ For when we live your peace, cap-tives will find re - lease,
3. Spir-it of God, bright Hands, e - ven in far - off lands you hold all the hu - man race in one warm em - brace. _____ No mat - ter where we go, you hold us to - geth - er so,
4. Spir-it of God, bright Flame, send us in your ho - ly name, the pow - er to heal, to share your love ev - ery - where. _____ We can - not fail or fall, or know de - feat at all,
5. Spir-it of God in all, we glad - ly hear your call, the life in our hands that sings, the power of your wings. _____ Born of your grace we rise, love shin-ing in our eyes,

Refrain

Al - le - lu - ia!

|1| |2|

Come, Spir - it, come! ___ come! _____

WORDS: Steve Garnaas-Holmes (Gen. 1:2; Matt. 3:16-17; Luke 3:22; Acts 2:1-4)
MUSIC: Steve Garnaas-Holmes

DOVE SONG
Irregular with Refrain

Holy Spirit, Come to Us

(Veni Sancte Spiritus)

2118

Repeat as desired.

Ho - ly Spir - it, come to us.
Ve - ni Sanc - te Spir - i - tus.

WORDS: Pentecost Sequence; adapt. by Jacques Berthier
MUSIC: Jacques Berthier

VENI SANCTE SPIRITUS
Irregular

© 1984 Les Presses de Taizé (France). Used by permission of GIA Publications, Inc.

Where the Spirit of the Lord Is

2119

Where the Spir-it of the Lord is, there is peace; where the

Spir - it of the Lord is, there is love. There is

com-fort in life's dark-est hour; there is light and life, there is

help and pow-er in the Spir-it, in the Spir-it of the Lord.

WORDS: Stephen R. Adams (2 Cor. 3:17)
MUSIC: Stephen R. Adams

ADAMS
Irregular

© 1973 Pilot Point Music (admin. by The Copyright Co., Nashville, TN)

2120 Like Miriam Who Danced to Praise

1. Like Mir - i - am who danced to praise the part-ing of the sea, and
2. Like proph-ets danc - ing to your tune be-fore a roy-al throne, or
3. Like those who danced with Je - sus Christ un - til his life was done, then

Da - vid who be - fore the ark danced on in ec - sta-sy, God,
march-ing to a free-dom song or stand-ing firm a-lone, God,
car - ried on the dance of love that he had just be-gun, God,

pour your spir - it in - to us; fill us with joy as well, that
send us vi - sions of your will; re - veal to us your Word, that
fill us with such loy - al - ty and pas-sion for their Friend, that

we may al - so join the dance and all your prais-es tell.
we may brave-ly dance our role and speak what we have heard.
we may fol - low in their steps to joy that has no end.

WORDS: Mary Nelson Keithahn (Exod. 15:19-21; 2 Sam. 6:1-19)
MUSIC: John D. Horman

FAITH DANCE
86.86 D

O Holy Spirit, Root of Life

2121

1. O Ho - ly Spir - it, Root of life, Cre - at - or,
2. E - ter - nal Vig - or, sav - ing One, you free us
3. O ho - ly wis - dom, soar - ing power, en - com - pass

cleans - er of all things, a - noint our wounds, a -
by your liv - ing Word, be - com - ing flesh to
us with wings un - furled, and car - ry us, en -

wak - en us with lus - trous move - ment of your wings.
wear our pain, and all cre - a - tion is re - stored.
cir - cling all, a - bove, be - low, and through the world.

WORDS: Jean Janzen, based on the writings of Hildegard of Bingen (12th cent.)   PUER NOBIS NASCITUR
        (John 1:14; Rom. 8:22-23)   LM
MUSIC: Trier manuscript (15th cent.); adapt. by Michael Praetorius; harm. by George R. Woodward

2122   She Comes Sailing on the Wind

Refrain

She comes sail-ing on the wind, her wings flash-ing in the sun; on a jour-ney just be-gun, she flies on.

And in the pas-sage of her flight, her song rings out through the night, full of laugh-ter, full of light, she flies on.

Fine

1. _____ Si-lent wa-ters rock-ing on the morn-ing of our
2. _____ Man-y were the dream-ers whose eyes were giv-en
3. To a gen-tle girl in Gal-i-lee, a gen-tle breeze she
4. _____ Fly-ing to the riv-er, she wait-ed cir-cling
5. Long af-ter the deep dark-ness that fell up-on the

birth, like an emp-ty cra-dle wait-ing to be
sight when the Spir-it filled their dreams with life and
came, a whis-per soft-ly call-ing in the
high a- bove the child now grown so full of
world, af-ter dawn re-turned in flame of ris-ing

filled. _____ And from the heart of God the Spir-it
form. _____ _____ Des-erts turned to gar-dens, bro-ken
dark, _____ the prom-ise of a child of peace whose
grace. _____ As he rose up from the wa-ter, she swept
sun, _____ the Spir-it touched the earth a-gain, a-

moved up-on the earth, like a moth-er breath-ing
hearts found new de-light, and then down the a-ges
reign would nev-er end, Ma-ry sang the Spir-it
down from the sky, and she car-ried him a-
gain, her wings un-furled, bring-ing life in wind and

WORDS: Gordon Light (Gen. 1:2; Matt. 3:16-17; Mark 1:10-11; Luke 1:26-56; 3:22; Acts 2:1-4) SHE FLIES ON
MUSIC: Gordon Light   Irregular with Refrain
© 1985 Common Cup Co.

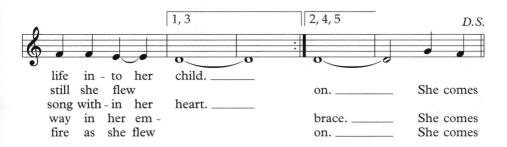

| 1, 3 | 2, 4, 5 | D.S. |

life in - to her child. _____
still she flew on. _____ She comes
song with - in her heart. _____
way in her em - brace. _____ She comes
fire as she flew on. _____ She comes

Spirit, Now Live in Me 2123

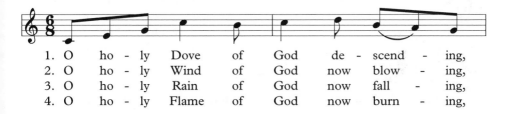

1. O ho - ly Dove of God de - scend - ing,
2. O ho - ly Wind of God now blow - ing,
3. O ho - ly Rain of God now fall - ing,
4. O ho - ly Flame of God now burn - ing,

you are the love that knows no end - ing,
you are the seed that God is sow - ing,
you make the Word of God en - thrall - ing,
you are the power of Christ re - turn - ing,

all of our shat - tered dreams you're mend - ing:
you are the life that starts us grow - ing:
you are that in - ner voice now call - ing:
you are the an - swer to our yearn - ing:

Spir - it, now live in me. A - men.

WORDS: Bryan Jeffery Leech (Matt. 3:16)
MUSIC: Bryan Jeffery Leech

SPIRIT, NOW LIVE IN ME
99.96

2124 Come, O Holy Spirit, Come
(Wa Wa Wa Emimimo)

Leader

Ho - ly Spir - it, come.
E - mi - o - lo - ye.

All

Come, O Ho - ly Spir - it, come,
Wa wa wa E - mi - mi - mo,

al - might - y Spir - it, come.
A - lag - ba - ra - me - ta.

Come, al - might - y Spir - it, come,
Wa wa wa A - lag - ba - ra,

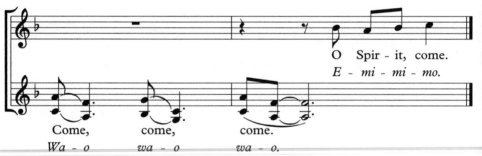

O Spir - it, come.
E - mi - mi - mo.

Come, come, come.
Wa - o wa - o wa - o.

WORDS: Original Yoruba; English trans. by I-to Loh
MUSIC: Trad. Yoruba as taught by Samuel Solanke (Nigeria)

WA EMIMIMO
Irregular

English trans. © 1995 General Board of Global Ministries, GBGMusik

2125 Come, Holy Spirit

Part 2 (descant)

Hear us call - ing,

Part 1 (melody)

Come, Ho - ly Spir - it. Come, Ho - ly

WORDS: Mark Foreman
MUSIC: Mark Foreman

FOREMAN
Irregular

© 1982 Mercy/Vineyard Publishing

2126

All Who Hunger

1. All who hun-ger, gath-er glad-ly; ho-ly man-na
2. All who hun-ger, nev-er strang-ers; seek-er, be a
3. All who hun-ger, sing to-geth-er; Je-sus Christ is

is our bread. Come from wil-der-ness and wan-dering.
wel-come guest. Come from rest-less-ness and roam-ing.
liv-ing bread. Come from lone-li-ness and long-ing.

Here, in truth, we will be fed. You that yearn for
Here, in joy, we keep the feast. We that once were
Here, in peace, we have been led. Blest are those who

days of full-ness, all a-round us is our food.
lost and scat-tered in com-mu-nion's love have stood.
from this ta-ble live their lives in grat-i-tude.

WORDS: Sylvia G. Dunstan (Exod. 16:13-15; Ps. 34:8; John 4:10; 1 Cor. 5:8)
MUSIC: William Moore

HOLY MANNA
87.87 D

Words © 1991 GIA Publications, Inc.

Taste and see the grace e - ter - nal. Taste and see that God is good.

Come and See
(Kyrie)
2127

1. "Come and see,   come and see,   I am the way and the truth," said he.
2.   Ky - ri - e,   Ky - ri - e,   Ky - ri - e   e - le - i - son.

"Fol-low me,   fol-low me, come as   a child, O come and see."__ *(to 2.)*
Chris - te,   Chris - te,   Chris - te   e - le - i - son. __ *(to 3.)*

Part 2 (descant)

3. Chris - te,*   Chris - te,   a - do - ra - mus te.

Part 1 (melody)

(2.) Ky - ri - e,*   Ky - ri - e,   Ky - ri - e   e - le - i - son.

Al - le - lu - ia,   Ky - ri - e   e - le - i - son.

Chris - te,   Chris - te,   Chris - te   e - le - i - son.

Translation: Christ, we adore you. Alleluia, Lord have mercy.
Lord, have mercy. Christ, have mercy.

WORDS: Marilyn Houser Hamm (John 1:35-51; 14:6)   MH KYRIE
MUSIC: Marilyn Houser Hamm   Irregular

GRACE

2128 Come and Find the Quiet Center

1. Come and find the qui-et cen-ter in the crowd-ed life we
2. Si-lence is a friend who claims us, cools the heat and slows the
3. In the Spir-it let us trav-el, o-pen to each oth-er's

lead, find the room for hope to en-ter, find the
pace, God it is who speaks and names us, knows our
pain, let our loves and fears un-rav-el, cel-e-

frame where we are freed: Clear the cha-os and the
be-ing, touch-es base, mak-ing space with-in our
brate the space we gain: There's a place for deep-est

clut-ter, clear our eyes that we can see all the
think-ing, lift-ing shades to show the sun, rais-ing
dream-ing, there's a time for heart to care, in the

things that real-ly mat-ter, be at peace, and sim-ply be.
cour-age when we're shrink-ing, find-ing scope for faith be-gun.
Spir-it's live-ly schem-ing there is al-ways room to spare.

WORDS: Shirley Erena Murray
MUSIC: Attr. to B. F. White

BEACH SPRING
87.87 D

Words © 1992 Hope Publishing Co.

2129 I Have Decided to Follow Jesus

1. I have de-cid-ed to fol-low Je-sus, I have de-
cid-ed to fol-low Je-sus, I have de-cid-ed to fol-low

2. The world behind me, the cross before me ...
3. Though none go with me, still I will follow ...

WORDS: Anon.
MUSIC: Anon.

ASSAM
10 10.10 8

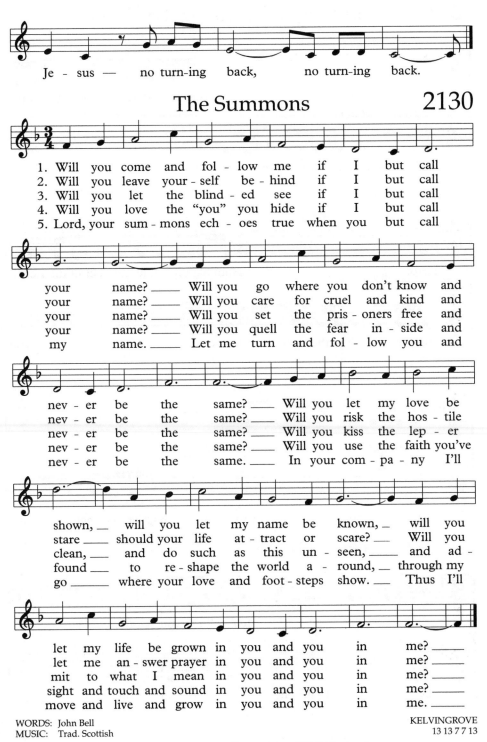

The Summons

2130

Je - sus — no turn-ing back, no turn-ing back.

1. Will you come and fol - low me if I but call
2. Will you leave your - self be - hind if I but call
3. Will you let the blind - ed see if I but call
4. Will you love the "you" you hide if I but call
5. Lord, your sum - mons ech - oes true when you but call

your name? ___ Will you go where you don't know and
your name? ___ Will you care for cruel and kind and
your name? ___ Will you set the pris - oners free and
your name? ___ Will you quell the fear in - side and
my name. ___ Let me turn and fol - low you and

nev - er be the same? ___ Will you let my love be
nev - er be the same? ___ Will you risk the hos - tile
nev - er be the same? ___ Will you kiss the lep - er
nev - er be the same? ___ Will you use the faith you've
nev - er be the same. ___ In your com - pa - ny I'll

shown, __ will you let my name be known, __ will you
stare ___ should your life at - tract or scare? ___ Will you
clean, __ and do such as this un - seen, ___ and ad -
found ___ to re - shape the world a - round, __ through my
go ___ where your love and foot - steps show. __ Thus I'll

let my life be grown in you and you in me? ___
let me an - swer prayer in you and you in me? ___
mit to what I mean in you and you in me? ___
sight and touch and sound in you and you in me? ___
move and live and grow in you and you in me. ___

WORDS: John Bell
MUSIC: Trad. Scottish

KELVINGROVE
13 13 7 7 13

2131 Humble Thyself in the Sight of the Lord

Part 2 (descant)

Hum-ble thy-self in the sight of the

Part 1 (melody)

Hum-ble thy-self in the sight of the Lord.

Lord.

Hum-ble thy-self in the sight of the Lord,

Hum-ble thy-self in the sight of the Lord,

and

and he shall lift you up,

he shall lift you up, high-er and high - er, and

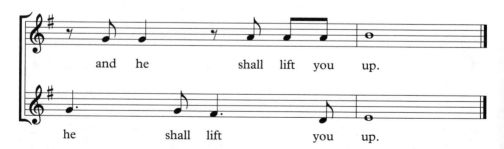

and he shall lift you up.

he shall lift you up.

WORDS: Bob Hudson (James 4:10)
MUSIC: Bob Hudson

HUMBLE THYSELF
Irregular

Come, Ye Disconsolate

1. Come, ye dis-con-so-late, wher-e'er ye lan-guish,
   Come to the mer-cy seat, fer-vent-ly kneel.
   Here bring your wound-ed hearts, here tell your an-guish;
   Earth has no sor-row that heaven can-not heal.

2. Joy of the des-o-late, Light of the stray-ing,
   Hope of the pen-i-tent, fade-less and pure!
   Here speaks the Com-fort-er, ten-der-ly say-ing,
   "Earth has no sor-row that heaven can-not cure."

3. Here see the Bread of Life; see wa-ters flow-ing
   Forth from the throne of God, pure from a-bove.
   Come to the feast of love; come, ev-er know-ing
   Earth has no sor-row but heaven can re-move.

WORDS: Thomas Moore; alt. by Thomas Hastings
MUSIC: Samuel Webbe Sr.

CONSOLATOR
11 10.11 10

2133 Give Me a Clean Heart

Give me a clean heart so I may serve thee. Lord, fix my heart so that I may be used by thee. For I'm not wor - thy of all those bless - ings. Give me a clean heart, _____ and I'll fol - low thee. _____

WORDS: Margaret P. Douroux (Ps. 51:10)
MUSIC: Margaret P. Douroux

DOUROUX
Irregular

© 1970 Margaret P. Douroux

2134 Forgive Us, Lord
(Perdón, Señor)

Leader

1. For griev-ance and in - jus - tice:
2. For weak-ness and trans-gres - sion:
3. In your e - ter - nal mer - cy:

1. *Por tan - tas in - jus - ti - cias:*
2. *Por to - das nues-tras fal - tas:*
3. *En tu mi - se - ri - cor - dia:*

All   *Fine*

For - give us, Lord.   For -
Per - dón, Se - ñor.   *Per -*

WORDS: Jorge Lockward; English trans. by Raquel Mora Martínez (Ps. 51:1-3)
MUSIC: Jorge Lockward

CONFESIÓN
4.74.74

© 1996 Abingdon Press (admin. by The Copyright Co., Nashville, TN)

D.C.

A - loof-ness and in - dif-ference:
Re - sis-tance and re - bel - lion:
In your sus - tain-ing grace:
Por tan-ta in - di - fe - ren - cia:
Por nues - tra re - bel - dí - a:
en tu di - vi - na gra - cia:

D.C.

give us, Lord.
dón, Se - ñor.

For-give us, Lord.
Per - dón, Se - ñor.

When Cain Killed Abel 2135

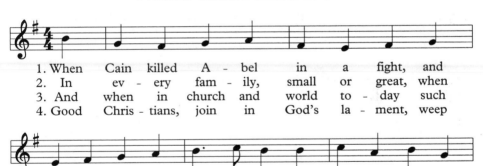

1. When Cain killed A - bel in a fight, and
2. In ev - ery fam - ily, small or great, when
3. And when in church and world to - day such
4. Good Chris - tians, join in God's la - ment, weep

Ja - cob stole an - oth - er's right, when Jo - seph's broth - ers
jeal - ou - sy twists love to hate, and ri - vals turn to
feel - ings still come in - to play, when broth-ers, sis - ters
now and mourn, be pen - i - tent, and pray to God: For -

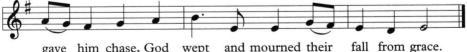

gave him chase, God wept and mourned their fall from grace.
en - e - mies, God weeps at our hos - til - i - ties.
stand a - part, God weeps for ev - ery bro - ken heart.
give us all. Re - store us as be - fore the fall.

WORDS: Mary Nelson Keithahn (Gen. 4:8-10; 27; 37)
MUSIC: John D. Horman

AFTER THE FALL
LM

Words © 1998, music © 2000 Abingdon Press (admin. by The Copyright Co., Nashville, TN)

2136

Out of the Depths

1. Out of the depths, O God, we call to you.
2. Out of the depths of fear, O God, we speak.
3. God of the lov - ing heart, we praise your name.

*Wounds of the past re - main, af - fect - ing all we do.
Break - ing the si - lenc - es, the sear - ing truth we seek.
Dance through our lives and loves; a - noint with Spir - it flame.

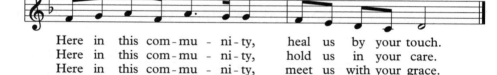

Fac - ing our lives, we need your love so much.
Safe a - mong friends, our grief and rage we share.
Your light il - lu - mines each fa - mil - iar face.

Here in this com - mu - ni - ty, heal us by your touch.
Here in this com - mu - ni - ty, hold us in your care.
Here in this com - mu - ni - ty, meet us with your grace.

*Ruth Duck has provided the following words that may be substituted for those who are seriously ill:
Free us from fear of death, our faith and hope renew ...

or, for those who have been abused:
Wounds of abuse remain, affecting all we do ...

WORDS: Ruth Duck (Ps. 130:1)
MUSIC: Robert J. Batastini

FENNVILLE
10 12.10 12

Words © 1988 and music © 1994 GIA Publications, Inc.

2137

Would I Have Answered When You Called?

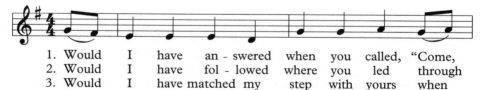

1. Would I have an - swered when you called, "Come,
2. Would I have fol - lowed where you led, through
3. Would I have matched my step with yours when
4. O Christ, I can - not search my heart through

WORDS: Herman G. Stuempfle Jr. (Matt. 4:12-23; 26:56; Mark 1:16-20; 14:50; Luke 5:1-11)
MUSIC: Trad. English melody

KINGSFOLD
CMD

Words © 1997 GIA Publications, Inc.

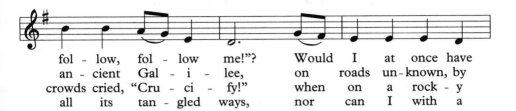

fol - low, fol - low me!"?   Would I at once have
an - cient Gal - i - lee,   on roads un-known, by
crowds cried, "Cru - ci - fy!"   when on a rock - y
all its tan - gled ways,   nor can I with a

left be - hind both work and fam - i -
ways un - tried, be - yond se - cu - ri -
hill I saw a cross a - gainst the
cer - tain mind my stead - fast - ness ap -

ly? Or would the old, fa - mil - iar round have
ty? Or would I soon have hur - ried back where
sky? Or would I too have slipped a - way and
praise. I on - ly pray that when you call, "Come,

held me by its claim and kept the spark with -
home and com - fort drew, where truth you taught would
left you there a - lone, a dy - ing king with
fol - low, fol - low me!" you'll give me strength be -

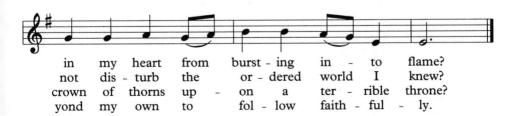

in my heart from burst - ing in - to flame?
not dis - turb the or - dered world I knew?
crown of thorns up - on a ter - rible throne?
yond my own to fol - low faith - ful - ly.

2138 Sunday's Palms Are Wednesday's Ashes

1. *Sun-day's palms are Wednes-day's ash - es as an -
2. We have failed to love our neigh - bors, their of -
3. We are hast - y to judge oth - ers, blind to

oth - er Lent be - gins; thus we kneel be - fore our
fenc - es to for - give, have not lis - tened to their
proof of hu-man need; and our lack of un - der -

Mak - er in con - tri - tion for our
trou - bles, nor have cared just how they
stand - ing dem - on - strates our in - ner

sins. We have marred bap - tis - mal pledg - es, in re -
live, we are jeal - ous, proud, im - pa - tient, lov - ing
greed; we have wast - ed earth's re - sourc - es; want and

bel - lion gone a - stray; now, re - turn - ing, seek for -
o - ver - much our things; may the yield - ing of our
suf - fering we've ig - nored; come and cleanse us, then re -

give - ness; grant us par - don, God, this day!
fail - ings be our Len - ten of - fer - ings.
store us; make new hearts with - in us, Lord!

*The first line of the hymn recalls the custom of burning remaining palm leaves of the previous year to form the ashes for this observance.

WORDS: Rae E. Whitney
MUSIC: Attr. to B. F. White

BEACH SPRING
87.87 D

Words © 1991 Selah Publishing Co., Inc.

REPENTANCE, *see further:*

2275   Kyrie (Dvořák/Schram)
2277   Lord, Have Mercy

Oh, I Know the Lord's Laid His Hands on Me

2139

Refrain

All

Oh, I know the Lord, I know the Lord,

I know the Lord's laid his hands on me. Oh, hands on me.

Leader

1. Did ev-er you see the like be-fore?
   King Je-sus preach-ing to the poor!
2. Oh, was-n't that a hap-py day
   when Je-sus washed my sins a-way!
3. ___ Some seek the Lord and don't seek him right;
   they fool all day and pray at night,
4. ___ My Lord's done just what he said;
   he's healed the sick and raised the dead;

All

I know the Lord's laid his hands on me; hands on me. Oh,

WORDS: African American spiritual
MUSIC: African American spiritual

I KNOW
Irregular with Refrain

2140   Since Jesus Came into My Heart

1. What a wonderful change in my life has been wrought
2. I have ceased from my wandering and going astray,
3. I'm possessed of a hope that is steadfast and sure,
4. There's a light in the valley of death now for me,
5. I shall go there to dwell in that City, I know,

since Jesus came into my heart!

I have
And my
And no
And the
And I'm

light in my soul for which long I had sought,
sins, which were many, are all washed away,
dark clouds of doubt now my pathway obscure,
gates of the City beyond I can see,
happy, so happy, as onward I go,

since

Refrain

Jesus came into my heart!   Since Jesus came into my
                            Since Jesus came in, came

WORDS: R. H. McDaniel
MUSIC: Charles H. Gabriel

McDANIEL
12 8.12 8 with Refrain

heart, since Je-sus came in-to my
in-to my heart, since Je-sus came in, came

heart, floods of joy o'er my soul like the
in-to my heart,

sea bil-lows roll, since Je-sus came in-to my heart.

There's a Song 2141

1. There's a song of *love in my heart; *love is a gift from Je-sus.

There's a song of *love in my heart; *love is a gift from God.

Al - le - lu - ia! *Love in my heart is sing-ing prais-es.

Al - le - lu - ia! *Love is a gift from God.

*2. Peace 3. Faith 4. Hope 5. Joy

WORDS: Handt Hanson
MUSIC: Handt Hanson

HANSON
87.86.49.46

© 1996 Changing Church Forum

GRACE

2142
Blessed Quietness

1. Joys are flow - ing like a riv - er, since the
2. Bring-ing life and health and glad - ness all a -
3. Like the rain that falls from heav - en, like the
4. See, a fruit - ful field is grow - ing, bless - ed
5. What a won - der - ful sal - va - tion, when we

Com - fort - er has come; Christ a - bides with us for -
round, this heaven - ly Guest ban-ished un - be - lief and
sun - light from the sky, so the Spir - it, too, is
fruit of righ - teous - ness; and the streams of life are
al - ways see Christ's face, what a per - fect hab - i -

ev - er, makes the trust - ing heart a home.
sad - ness, changed our wea - ri - ness to rest.
giv - en, com - ing on us from on high.
flow - ing in the lone - ly wil - der - ness.
ta - tion, what a qui - et rest - ing place.

Refrain

Bless-ed qui-et-ness, ho - ly qui-et-ness, what a s -

WORDS: Manie P. Ferguson (Matt. 8:24-26; John 14:16-19)
MUSIC: W. S. Marshall; arr. by J. Jefferson Cleveland and Verolga Nix

BLESSED QUIETNESS
87.87 with Refrain

O Lord, Your Tenderness — 2143

sur - ance in my soul. On the storm-y sea, Je-sus

speaks to me, and the bil - lows cease to roll.

O Lord, your ten - der - ness, melt-ing all my

bit - ter - ness; O Lord, I re - ceive your love. ___

O Lord, your love - li - ness, chang-ing my un -

worth - i - ness; O Lord, I re - ceive your love. ___

O Lord, I re - ceive your love; ___

O Lord, I re - ceive your love. ___

WORDS: Graham Kendrick (Isa. 61:3)
MUSIC: Graham Kendrick

© 1986 ThankYou Music.

YOUR TENDERNESS
Irregular

2144

In All Our Grief

1. In all our grief and fear we turn to you. O God, you
2. Help us to put a - side the an - gry word, the clench-ing
3. You did not e - ven spare your on - ly Son. He lived our
4. God, when we suf - fer all that we can bear, then let us

know all that we think or do, You know the pain we
fist, the wish and will to hurt. Teach us the way in
griefs and bore all e - vil done, but through his cross, re -
know that you in truth are near and will not leave us

put each oth - er through.
which love best is served.
demp - tion was be - gun.
lost in all our fear.

Lord, have mer - cy.

Christ, have mer - cy. Lord, grant us peace.

WORDS: Sylvia G. Dunstan
MUSIC: Charles R. Anders

FREDERICKTOWN
10 10 10.4 4 4

Words © 1991 GIA Publications, Inc.; music © 1978 *Lutheran Book of Worship* (admin. by Augsburg Fortress)

2145 God's Great Love Is So Amazing!

1. God's great love is so a - maz - ing! See— a
2. God in love is al - ways seek - ing! See— a
3. God keeps wait-ing, search-ing, yearn - ing! See— a

WORDS: Carolyn Winfrey Gillette (Luke 15)
MUSIC: Charles Crozat Converse

CONVERSE
87.87 D

Words © 1999 Carolyn Winfrey Gillette from *Gifts of Love: New Hymns for Today's Worship*

shep-herd with his flocks! Nine - ty - nine are safe - ly
wom - an with her broom! For a sin - gle coin she's
fa - ther's heart-felt joy! Thank - ful for his son's re -

graz - ing; one is lost a - mong the rocks. That good
sweep - ing ev - ery cor-ner of the room. When it's
turn - ing, he runs out to greet his boy. To the

shep-herd goes and search - es till he finds the one a - stray.
found she calls each neigh - bor, tell - ing friends from all a - round.
an - gry old - er broth - er, hear the fa - ther's pa-tient call.

So God says to fill our church-es with the ones who've lost their way.
So God says to search and la - bor till God's pre - cious ones are found.
So God says to love each oth - er, for in Christ God loves us all.

2146 His Eye Is on the Sparrow

1. Why should I feel dis-cour-aged? Why should the shad-ows
2. "Let not your heart be trou-bled," his ten-der word I
3. When-ev-er I am tempt-ed, when-ev-er clouds a-

come? Why should my heart be lone-ly
hear, and rest-ing on his good-ness,
rise, when song gives place to sigh-ing,

and long for heaven and home, When Je-sus is my
I lose my doubts and fears; though by the path he
when hope with-in me dies, I draw the clo-ser

por-tion? My con-stant friend is he:
lead-eth but one step I may see: ⎫ His eye is on the
to him, from care he sets me free: ⎭

spar-row, and I know he watch-es me; his eye is on the

spar-row, and I know he watch-es me. I sing be-cause I'm

hap-py, (I'm hap-py,) I sing be-cause I'm free, (I'm free,) for his

WORDS: Civilla Martin (Luke 12:6-7; John 14:1)
MUSIC: Charles H. Gabriel

SPARROW
Irregular with Refrain

Yes, God Is Real 2147

1. There are some things I may not know, there are some
2. Some folks may doubt, some folks may scorn, all can de -
3. I can - not tell just how you felt when Je - sus

plac - es I can't go, but I am sure of this one
sert and leave me a - lone, but as for me I'll take God's
took your sins a - way, but since that day, yes, since that

thing, that God is real for I can feel God deep with - in.
part, for God is real and I can feel God in my heart.
hour, God has been real for I can feel God's ho - ly power.

Refrain

Yes, God is real, real in my soul; yes, God is real for God has

washed and made me whole; God's love for me is like pure

gold, yes, God is real for I can feel God in my soul.

WORDS: Kenneth Morris
MUSIC: Kenneth Morris

YES, GOD IS REAL
88.8 12 with Refrain

2148 Over My Head

Refrain

O-ver my head, I hear mu-sic in the air; o-ver my head, I hear mu-sic in the air; o-ver my head, I hear mu-sic in the air; there must be a God some-where.

Fine

Leader

1. Oh, when the world is si-lent, _____ oh,
2. And when I'm feel-ing lone-ly, _____ and
3. Now when I think on Je-sus, _____ now

All

Hmm, I hear mu-sic in the air;

WORDS: African American spiritual
MUSIC: African American spiritual; arr. by John Bell, alt.

MUSIC IN THE AIR
Irregular with Refrain

when the world is si - lent, _____ oh,
when I'm feel-ing lone - ly, _____ and
when I think on Je - sus, _____ now

hmm, I hear mu - sic in the air;

when the world is si - lent, _____
when I'm feel-ing lone - ly, _____
when I think on Je - sus, _____

hmm I hear mu - sic in the air;

D.C.

there must be a God some - where.

D.C.

there must be a God some - where.

2149 Living for Jesus

1. Liv-ing for Je-sus a life that is true,
2. Liv-ing for Je-sus who died in my place,
3. Liv-ing for Je-sus wher-ev-er I am,
4. Liv-ing for Je-sus through earth's lit-tle while,

striv-ing to please him in all that I do,
bear-ing on Cal-vary my sin and dis-grace,
do-ing each du-ty in his ho-ly name,
my dear-est trea-sure, the light of his smile,

yield-ing al-le-giance, glad-heart-ed and free,
such love con-strains me to an-swer his call,
will-ing to suf-fer af-flic-tion or loss,
seek-ing the lost ones he died to re-deem,

this is the path-way of bless-ing for me.
fol-low his lead-ing and give him my all.
deem-ing each tri-al a part of my cross.
bring-ing the wea-ry to find rest in him.

WORDS: T. O. Chisolm
MUSIC: C. Harold Lowden

LIVING FOR JESUS
10 10.10 10 with Refrain

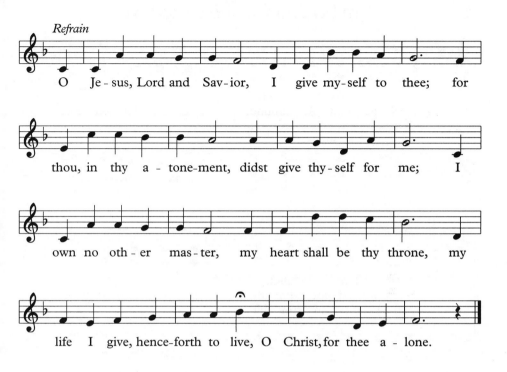

Refrain

O Je-sus, Lord and Sav-ior, I give my-self to thee; for thou, in thy a-tone-ment, didst give thy-self for me; I own no oth-er mas-ter, my heart shall be thy throne, my life I give, hence-forth to live, O Christ, for thee a-lone.

Lord, Be Glorified 2150

1. In our lives, Lord, be glo-ri-fied, be glo-ri-fied.
   (my)   (life)
In our lives, Lord, be glo-ri-fied to-day.
(my)   (life)

2. In our homes ...
3. In your church ...
4. In your world ...

WORDS: Bob Kilpatrick (John 15:8; 1 Cor. 6:20; 2 Cor. 9:13; 2 Thess. 1:11-20)
MUSIC: Bob Kilpatrick

LORD, BE GLORIFIED
Irregular

GRACE

2151   I'm So Glad Jesus Lifted Me

1. I'm   so   glad,
2. Sa - tan had me bound,
3. When I was in trou - ble,

       Je - sus lift - ed me,

I'm   so   glad,
Sa - tan had me bound,
when I was in trou - ble,

       Je - sus lift - ed me,

I'm   so   glad,
Sa - tan had me bound,
when I was in trou - ble,

       Je - sus lift - ed me,   sing - ing

glo - ry, hal - le - lu - jah,   Je - sus lift - ed me.

WORDS: African American spiritual
MUSIC: African American spiritual

I'M SO GLAD
Irregular

Change My Heart, O God

2152

Change my heart, O God, __ make it ev-er true. __
__ Change my heart, O God, __
may I be like you. __ You are the
Pot - ter, I am the clay. __
Mold me and make me, this is what I
pray. Change my heart, O God, __
make it ev-er true. _ Change my heart, O God, __
__ may I be like you. __

WORDS: Eddie Espinosa (Isa. 64:8)
MUSIC: Eddie Espinosa

CHANGE MY HEART
Irregular

Transform Us

1. Trans-form us as you, trans - fig - ured,
2. Trans-form us as you, trans - fig - ured,
3. Trans-form us as you, trans - fig - ured,

stood a - part on Ta - bor's height.
once spoke with those ho - ly ones.
would not stay with - in a shrine.

Lead us up our sa - cred moun - tains,
We, sur - round - ed by the wit - ness
Keep us from our great temp - ta - tion—

search us with re - veal - ing light.
of those saints whose work is done,
time and truth we quick - ly bind.

Lift us from where we have fall -
live in this world as your Bod -
Lead us down those dai - ly path -

en, full of ques - tions, filled with fright.
y, chos - en daugh-ters, chos - en sons.
ways where our love is not con - fined.

WORDS: Sylvia G. Dunstan (Matt. 17:1-8; Mark 9:2-8; Luke 9:28-36)
MUSIC: French, 17th cent.
Words © 1991 GIA Publications, Inc.

PICARDY
87.87.87

Please Enter My Heart, Hosanna   2154

1., 3. Please en - ter my heart, ho - san - na. O
(2., 4. O) please hear my prayer ho - san - na, these

please lead my life to - day.
words that I need to say.

Gen - tle Lamb of God, the Christ, the a - noint - ed one, won't you

|1, 3| en - ter my heart to - day? 2., 4. O ||2, 4| stay? O come, Je - sus,

come. Ho - san - na! Ho - san - na! O

Last time to Coda   D.S. al Coda

come, Je - sus, come to - day. 3. Please

CODA

come. Ho - san - na! Ho - san - na! O come, Je - sus,

come to - day, _____ come to stay. _____

WORDS: Cathy Townley
MUSIC: Cathy Townley

ENTER MY HEART
Irregular

© 1997 Abingdon Press (admin. by The Copyright Co., Nashville, TN)

Blest Are They

1. Blest are they, the poor in spir - it; theirs is the
2. Blest are they, the low - ly ones; they shall in -
3. Blest are they who show mer - cy; mer - cy
4. Blest are they who seek peace; they are the
5. Blest are you who suf - fer hate, all be -

king-dom of God. _____ Blest are they,
her - it the earth. _____ Blest are they who
shall be theirs. _____ Blest are they, the
chil - dren of God. _____ Blest are they who
cause of me. ___ Re - joice and be glad,

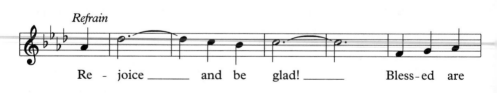

full of sor - row; they shall be con - soled. ___
hun - ger and thirst; they shall have their fill. ___
pure of heart; they shall see God! ___
suf - fer in faith; the glo - ry of God is theirs. ___
yours is the king-dom. Shine for all to see. ___

Refrain

Re - joice _____ and be glad! _____ Bless-ed are

you, ho - ly are you. Re - joice _____ and be glad! ___

___ Yours is the king-dom of God! _____

WORDS: David Haas (Matt. 5:3-16)
MUSIC: David Haas

BLEST ARE THEY
Irregular with Refrain

Give Peace
(Da Pacem Cordium)

2156

Give peace to ev-ery heart. Give peace to ev-ery heart. Give
Da pa-cem cor-di-um. Da pa-cem cor-di-um. Da

peace, _____ Lord. Give peace, _____ Lord.
pa - cem. Da pa - cem.

May be sung as a canon. (A) may always be sung by the congregation if desired; soloists or the choir singing (B) and (C).

WORDS: Anon.
MUSIC: Jacques Berthier and the Taizé Community

DA PACEM
Irregular

© 1984 Les Presses de Taizé (France). Used by permission of GIA Publications, Inc.

Come and Fill Our Hearts
(Confitemini Domino)

2157

Come and fill our hearts with your peace.
Con - fi - te - mi - ni Do - mi - no

You a-lone, O Lord, are ho - ly. Come and fill our hearts
quo - ni - am bo - nus. Con - fi - te - mi - ni

with your peace, Al - le - lu - ia!
Do - mi - no, Al - le - lu - ia!

WORDS: Jacques Berthier (Ps. 137)
MUSIC: Jacques Berthier

CONFITEMINI DOMINO
Irregular

© 1991 Les Presses de Taizé (France). Used by permission of GIA Publications, Inc.

2158 Just a Closer Walk with Thee

1. I am weak, but thou art strong;
2. Through this world of toil and snares,
3. When my fee-ble life is o'er,

Je - sus, keep me from all wrong;   I'll be sat-is-fied as
if I fal-ter, Lord, who cares?   Who with me my bur-den
time for me will be no more;   guide me gent-ly, safe-ly

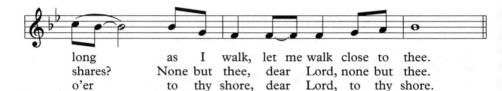

long as I walk, let me walk close to thee.
shares? None but thee, dear Lord, none but thee.
o'er to thy shore, dear Lord, to thy shore.

Refrain

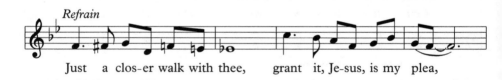

Just a clos-er walk with thee, grant it, Je-sus, is my plea,

dai - ly walk-ing close to thee: Let it be, dear Lord, let it be.

WORDS: Anon. (James 4:8)   CLOSER WALK
MUSIC: Anon.   Irregular with Refrain

2159 Jesus, Draw Me Close

Je - sus, draw me close, _ clos-er, Lord, to you. _

(For)

WORDS: Rick Founds (James 4:8)   DRAW ME CLOSE
MUSIC: Rick Founds   Irregular

1. Let the world a-round me fade a-way.

2. I de-sire to wor-ship and o-bey.

Into My Heart 2160

1. In - to my heart, in - to my heart, come
2. Out of my heart, out of my heart, shine

in - to my heart, Lord Je - sus; come in to-day, come
out of my heart, Lord Je - sus; shine out to-day, shine

in to stay; come in-to my heart, Lord Je - sus.
out al-way; shine out of my heart, Lord Je - sus.

WORDS: Harry D. Clarke; st. 2 anon.
MUSIC: Harry D. Clarke

INTO MY HEART
448.448

2161
To Know You More

1. To know you in all of your glo-ry, to
(2., 4. To) know you in all of your pow-er, to
(3. To) know you in all of your mer-cy, to

love you with all that I am. With all of my
trust you with all that I am. With all of my
serve you with all that I am. With all of my

1, 3

heart, Lord, this is my prayer: To know you
heart, Lord,
heart, Lord, this is my prayer: To know you

2, 4

more. 2. To
this is my prayer: To
more. 4. To

Second time to Coda ⊕   *D.S. al Coda*

know you more. 3. To

⊕ CODA

more. To know you more. _____

WORDS: Joe Horness (Phil. 3:10)
MUSIC: Joe Horness

TO KNOW YOU MORE
98.554

Grace Alone

1. Ev - ery prom - ise we can make, ev - ery prayer and
2. Ev - ery soul we long to reach, ev - ery heart we

step of faith, ev - ery dif - ference we will make
hope to teach, ev - ery - where we share his peace

is on - ly by his grace. Ev - ery moun - tain
is on - ly by his grace. Ev - ery lov - ing

we will climb, ev - ery ray of hope we shine,
word we say, ev - ery tear we wipe a - way,

ev - ery bless - ing left be - hind }
ev - ery sor - row turned to praise } is on - ly by his

Refrain

grace. Grace a - lone which God sup - plies, strength un -

known he will pro - vide. Christ in us our Cor - ner -

stone; we will go forth in grace a - lone.

WORDS: Scott Wesley Brown and Jeff Nelson (Eph. 2:8-10)
MUSIC: Scott Wesley Brown and Jeff Nelson

GRACE ALONE
Irregular with Refrain

GRACE

2163 He Who Began a Good Work in You

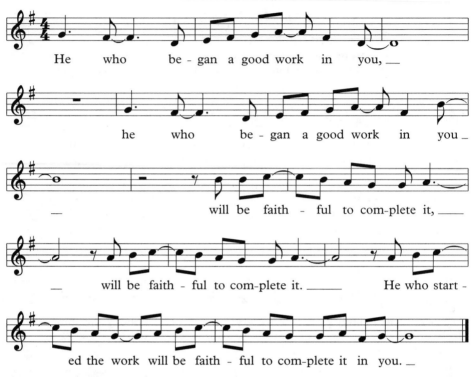

He who be-gan a good work in you, ___

he who be-gan a good work in you ___

___ will be faith-ful to com-plete it, ___

___ will be faith-ful to com-plete it. ___ He who start-

ed the work will be faith-ful to com-plete it in you. _

WORDS: Jon Mohr (Phil. 1:6)
MUSIC: Jon Mohr

A GOOD WORK
Irregular

© 1987 Jonathan Mark Music and Birdwing Music

2164 Sanctuary

Lord, pre-pare me to be a sanc-tu-ar-y, pure and

ho-ly, tried and true. With thanks-giv-ing, I'll be a

liv-ing sanc-tu-ar-y for you.

WORDS: John Thompson and Randy Scruggs
MUSIC: John Thompson and Randy Scruggs

SANCTUARY
Irregular

© 1982 Whole Armor/Full Armor Music (admin. by The Kruger Organization)

Cry of My Heart

It is the cry of my heart to fol - low you.

It is the cry of my heart to be close to you.

It is the cry of my heart to fol - low

all of the days of my life. _____

1. Teach me your ho - ly ways, __ O Lord, __
2. O - pen my eyes so I ____ can see the

so I can walk in your truth. __
won - der - ful things that you do. __

Teach me your ho - ly ways, __ O Lord, and make me
O - pen my heart up more __ and more, and make me

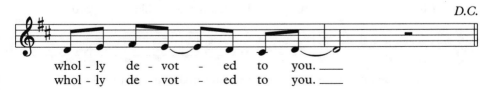

whol - ly de - vot - ed to you. __
whol - ly de - vot - ed to you. __

WORDS: Terry Butler (Ps. 25:4-5)
MUSIC: Terry Butler

CRY OF MY HEART
Irregular with Refrain

© 1991 Mercy/Vineyard Publishing Co.

2166   Christ Beside Me

1., 3. Christ be - side me, Christ be - fore me,
2. Christ on my right hand, Christ on my left hand,

Christ be - hind me — King of my heart; _____
Christ all a - round me — shield in the strife; _____

Christ with - in me, Christ be - low me,
Christ in my sleep - ing, Christ in my sit - ting,

Christ a - bove me — nev - er to part. _____
Christ in my ris - ing — light of my life. _____

WORDS: *St. Patrick's Breastplate;* adapt. by James Quinn
MUSIC: Trad. Gaelic melody

BUNESSAN
55.54 D

2167   More Like You

More like you, Je-sus, more like you.

Fill my heart with your de-sire to make me more like you.

More like you, Je-sus, more like you.

Fine

Touch my lips with ho - ly fire and make me more like you.

WORDS: Scott Wesley Brown
MUSIC: Scott Wesley Brown

MORE LIKE YOU
Irregular

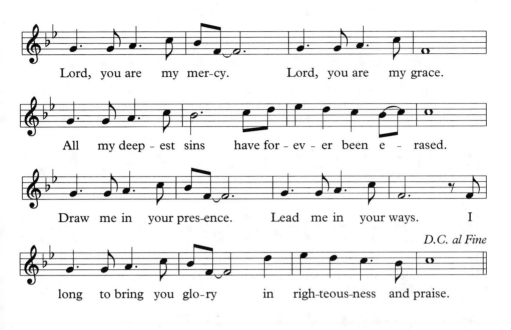

Lord, you are my mer-cy. Lord, you are my grace.

All my deep-est sins have for-ev-er been e-rased.

Draw me in your pres-ence. Lead me in your ways. I

D.C. al Fine

long to bring you glo-ry in righ-teous-ness and praise.

Love the Lord Your God — 2168

Love the Lord, your God, ____ with all your

heart. ____ Love the Lord, your God, ____ with

all your soul. ____ Love the Lord, your

God, ____ with all your mind. ____ Love the

Lord, your God, ____ with all that you are. ____

WORDS: Jean and Jim Strathdee (Deut. 6:5; Matt. 22:37; Mark 12:30; Luke 10:27) GREAT COMMANDMENT
MUSIC: Jean and Jim Strathdee Irregular

© 1991 Desert Flower Music

2169   God, How Can We Forgive

1. God, how can we for-give when bonds of love are torn?
2. When we have missed the mark, and tears of an-guish flow,
3. Who dares to throw the stone to damn an-oth-er's sin,

How can we rise and start a-new, our trust re - born?
how can you still re - lease our guilt, the debt we owe?
when you, while know-ing all our past, for-give a - gain?

When hu - man lov - ing fails and ev - ery hope is gone,
The o - cean depth of grace sur - pass - es all our needs.
No more we play the judge, for by your grace we live.

your love gives strength be - yond our own to face the dawn.
A priest who shares our hu - man pain, Christ in - ter - cedes.
As you, O God, for - give our sin, may we for - give.

WORDS: Ruth Duck (Matt. 6:12-15; 18:21-35; John 8:2-11)
MUSIC: Hebrew melody, *Sacred Harmony*; harm. from *Hymns Ancient and Modern*, alt.
Words © 1996 The Pilgrim Press

LEONI
66.84 D

God Made from One Blood

1. God made from one blood all the fam - ilies of earth,
2. We turn to you, God, with our thanks and our tears
3. We learn through our fam - ilies how close - ness and trust
4. Give, Lord, to each fam - ily in con - flict and storm
5. Then wid - en that wis - dom and grace to in - clude

the cir - cles of nur - ture that raised us from birth,
for all of the fam - ilies we've known through the years,
in - crease when our ac - tions are lov - ing and just.
a sense of your wis - dom and grace that trans - form
the rac - es and view-points our fam - ilies ex - clude

com - pan - ions who join us to walk through each stage
the in - ti - mate net - works on whom we de - pend
Yet fam - ilies have al - so dis - tort - ed their roles,
sharp an - ger to in - sight which strength - ens the heart
till peace in each home bears and nur - tures the bud

of child - hood and youth and a - dult - hood and age.
of par - ent and part - ner and room-mate and friend.
mis - treat - ing their mem - bers and bruis - ing their souls.
and makes clear the place where re - build - ing can start.
of peace shared by all you have made from one blood.

WORDS: Thomas H. Troeger (Acts 17:26)
MUSIC: Welsh folk melody

ST. DENIO
11 11.11 11

2171 Make Me a Channel of Your Peace

1. Make me a chan-nel of your peace. ___ Where
2. Make me a chan-nel of your peace. ___ Where
4. Make me a chan-nel of your peace. It

there is ha-tred, let me bring your love. ___ Where
there's de-spair in life, let me bring hope. ___ Where
is in par-don - ing that we are par - doned, ___ in

there is in - ju - ry, your par-don, Lord, ___ — and
there is dark - ness, ___ on - ly light, ___ — and
giv - ing of our - selves that we re - ceive, ___ and in

where there's doubt, true faith in you. ___
where there's sad - ness, ev - er joy. —
dy - ing that we're born to e-ter-nal life. —

3. Oh, Mas-ter, grant that I may nev - er seek ___ so

much to be con - soled as to con - sole. ___ To be

un - der-stood as to un - der - stand, ___ to be

loved as to love with all my soul. ___

WORDS: *Prayer of St. Francis;* adapt. by Sebastian Temple (Matt. 6:12-15)
MUSIC: Sebastian Temple

CHANNEL OF PEACE
Irregular

We Are Called

1. Come! Live in the light! _____ Shine with the
2. Come! O - pen your heart! _____ Show your
3. Sing! Sing a new song! _____ Sing of that

joy and the love of the Lord! We are called _____ to be
mer - cy to all those in fear! We are called _____ to be
great day when all will be one! God will reign, _____ and we'll

light for the king-dom, to live in the free - dom of the
hope for the hope-less so all ha - tred and blind-ness will
walk with each oth - er as sis - ters and broth-ers u -

Refrain

cit - y of God! _____
be no more! _____ We are called to act with
nit - ed in love! _____

jus-tice, _____ we are called to love ten - der - ly, _____

_ we are called to serve one an - oth-er, _____ to

walk hum - bly with God! _____

WORDS: David Haas (Mic. 6:8)
MUSIC: David Haas

WE ARE CALLED
Irregular with Refrain

2173   Shine, Jesus, Shine

Refrain

Shine, Je - sus, shine, _ fill this land with the Fa-ther's glo - ry,

blaze, Spir - it, blaze, _ set our hearts on fire;

flow, riv - er, flow, _ flood the na - tions with grace and mer-cy,

Fine

send forth your word, _ Lord, and let there be light.

1. Lord, the light of your love is shin - ing
2. Lord, I come to your awe - some pres - ence
3. As we gaze on your king - ly bright - ness,

in the midst of the dark - ness shin - ing;
from the shad - ows in - to your ra - di - ance;
so our fac - es dis - play your like - ness;

Je - sus, Light of the World, shine up - on us,
by the blood I may en - ter your bright - ness,
ev - er chang - ing from glo - ry to glo - ry,

set us free by the truth you now bring us.
search me, try me, con - sume all my dark - ness.
mir - rored here may our lives tell your sto - ry.

WORDS: Graham Kendrick (2 Cor. 4:6)
MUSIC: Graham Kendrick

SHINE, JESUS, SHINE
Irregular with Refrain

D.C.

Shine on me, shine on me.
Shine on me, shine on me.
Shine on me, shine on me.

What Does the Lord Require of You? 2174

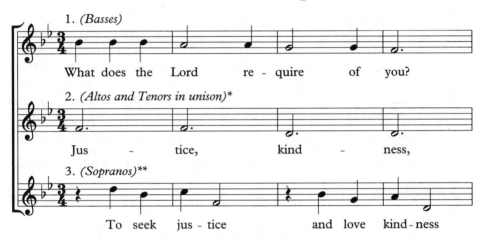

1. (Basses)

What does the Lord re - quire of you?

2. (Altos and Tenors in unison)*

Jus - tice, kind - ness,

3. (Sopranos)**

To seek jus - tice and love kind - ness

Repeat as desired.

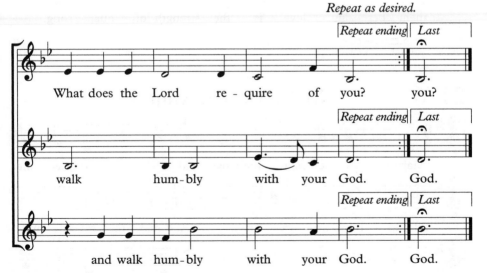

Repeat ending | Last

What does the Lord re - quire of you? you?

Repeat ending | Last

walk hum - bly with your God. God.

Repeat ending | Last

and walk hum - bly with your God. God.

*Enter on first repeat.
**Enter on second repeat.

WORDS: Jim Strathdee (Mic. 6:8)
MUSIC: Jim Strathdee

MOON
Irregular

© 1986 Desert Flower Music

2175

Together We Serve

1. To - geth - er we serve, u - nit - ed by love, in -
2. We seek to be - come a bea - con of hope, a
3. We wel-come the scarred, the wealth - y, the poor, the
4. To - geth - er, by grace, we wit - ness and work, re -

vit - ing God's world to the glo - ri - ous feast. We
lamp for the heart and a light for the feet. We
bus - y, the lone - ly, and all who need care. We
mem - ber - ing Je - sus, in whom we grow strong. To -

work and we pray through sor - row and joy, ex -
learn, year by year, to let love shine through un -
of - fer a home to those who will come, our
geth - er we serve in Spir - it and truth, re -

tend - ing your love to the last and the least.
til we see Christ in each per - son we meet.
hands quick to help, our hearts read - y to dare.
mem - ber - ing love is the strength of our song.

WORDS: Daniel Charles Damon
MUSIC: Daniel Charles Damon

SAN ANSELMO
55.11 D

© 1998 Hope Publishing Co.

2176

Make Me a Servant

Make me a ser-vant, hum-ble and meek, Lord, let me

lift up those who are weak. And may the prayer of my

heart al - ways be: Make me a ser-vant, make me a

WORDS: Kelly Willard (John 13:14-16)
MUSIC: Kelly Willard

MAKE ME A SERVANT
Irregular

© 1982 CCCM/Willing Heart Music (admin. by Maranatha! Music c/o The Copyright Co., Nashville, TN)

ser - vant, make me a ser - vant to - day. _____

Wounded World that Cries for Healing 2177

1. Wound - ed world that cries for heal - ing —
2. Through our na - tion's spent frus - tra - tion,
3. Hon - or those whose lov - ing spir - it

here we hold each oth - er's pain, wound - ed sys - tems,
through the cor - ri - dors of stress may there move a
nurs - es hope, re - stores and heals, towel and ba - sin

bruised and bleed - ing bear the load, the scars of strain;
kind - lier wis - dom all may feel, and all may bless;
used in ser - vice like the Christ who comes and kneels;

dol - lars ra - tion out com - pas - sion,
tax and tithe are for a pur - pose
in the tend - ing, in the mend - ing

hard de - ci - sions rule the day, Je - sus of the
shared to shield the poor and weak; past the symp-toms
may we see the right and fair, in our com - mon

heal - ing Spir - it, free us to an - oth - er way!
of our sick - ness let the voice of jus - tice speak.
quest for whole-ness heal each oth - er by our care.

WORDS: Shirley Erena Murray
MUSIC: Hal H. Hopson
© 1996 Hope Publishing Co.

HEALING SPIRIT
87.87 D

2178

Here Am I

1. Here am I, where un-der-neath the brid - ges
2. Here am I, with peo - ple in the line - up,
3. Here am I, where two or three are gath - ered,

in our win-ter cit - ies home-less peo-ple sleep. Here am I, where
anx-ious for a hand-out, ach - ing for a job. Here am I, when
read - y to be al - tered, shar - ing wine and bread. Here am I, where

in de - cay-ing hous - es lit - tle chil-dren shiv - er,
pen - sion-ers and strik - ers sing and march to - geth - er,
those who hear the preach - ing change their way of liv - ing,

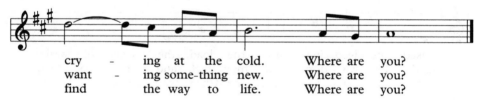

cry - ing at the cold. Where are you?
want - ing some-thing new. Where are you?
find the way to life. Where are you?

WORDS: Brian Wren (Matt. 25:31-46)
MUSIC: Daniel Charles Damon

STANISLAUS
37.65 D 3

Words © 1983 and music © 1995 Hope Publishing Co.

2179

Live in Charity
(Ubi Caritas)

Live in char - i - ty and stead - fast love,
U - bi ca - ri - tas et a - mor,

Stanzas included in other editions.

WORDS: 9th cent. Latin (1 Cor. 13:2-8)
MUSIC: Jacques Berthier and the Taizé Community

UBI CARITAS (TAIZÉ)
Irregular

© 1979 Les Presses de Taizé (France). Used by permission of GIA Publications, Inc.

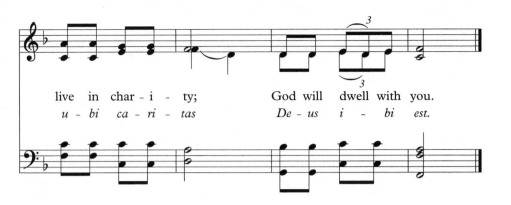

live in char - i - ty; God will dwell with you.
u - bi ca - ri - tas De - us i - bi est.

Why Stand So Far Away, My God? 2180

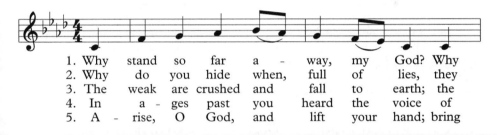

1. Why stand so far a - way, my God? Why
2. Why do you hide when, full of lies, they
3. The weak are crushed and fall to earth; the
4. In a - ges past you heard the voice of
5. A - rise, O God, and lift your hand; bring

hide in times of need? The proud, un - bri - dled,
mur - der and be - tray? They wait to pounce up -
wick - ed strut and preen. Why in these cruel, cha -
those the proud op - press. Re - mem - ber those who
jus - tice to the poor. Come, help us stop the

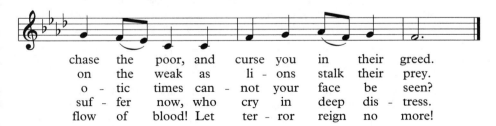

chase the poor, and curse you in their greed.
on the weak as li - ons stalk their prey.
o - tic times can - not your face be seen?
suf - fer now, who cry in deep dis - tress.
flow of blood! Let ter - ror reign no more!

WORDS: Ruth Duck (Ps. 10)   MORNING SONG
MUSIC: Wyeth's *Repository of Sacred Music, Part Second*   CM

Words © 1992 GIA Publications, Inc.

2181 We Need a Faith

1. We need a faith so col-or-blind, so
2. We need an eth-ic of re-spect, an
3. We need to act as well as speak, to
4. Come, Chris-tians, look for char-ac-ter and

free from time-worn lies, that when we look from
hon-est pledge of trust, that when we share the
see each oth-er's sweat, that as we la-bor
not for shade of skin, that as we rend the

face to face we see the eyes of God.
deep-est things we feel the warmth of God.
side by side we do the work of God.
walls of race we live the peace of God.

WORDS: John Thornburg
MUSIC: Jesse Seymour Irvine

CRIMOND
CM

Words © 1995 Abingdon Press (admin. by The Copyright Co., Nashville, TN)

2182 When God Restored Our Common Life

1. When God re-stored our com-mon life, our hope, our lib-er-
2. We went forth weep-ing, sow-ing seeds in hard, un-yield-ing
3. Great lib-er-at-ing God, we pray for all who are op-

ty, at first it seemed a pass-ing dream, a
soil; with laugh-ing hearts we car-ry home the
pressed. May those who long for what is right with

wak-ing fan-ta-sy. A shock of joy swept
fruit of all our toil. We praise the One who
jus-tice now be blest. We pray for those who

WORDS: Ruth Duck (Ps. 126)
MUSIC: USA folk melody, Walker's *Southern Harmony*

RESIGNATION
CMD

Words © 1992 Damean Music. Used by permission of GIA Publications, Inc.

o - ver us, for we had wept so long; the
gave the growth, with voic - es full and strong. The
mourn this day, and all who suf - fer wrong; may

seeds we wa-tered once with tears sprang up in-to a song.
seeds we wa-tered once with tears sprang up in-to a song.
seeds they wa - ter now with tears spring up in-to a song.

Unsettled World 2183

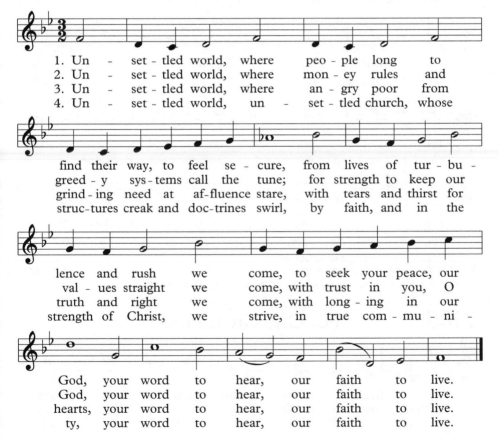

1. Un - set - tled world, where peo - ple long to
2. Un - set - tled world, where mon - ey rules and
3. Un - set - tled world, where an - gry poor from
4. Un - set - tled world, un - set - tled church, whose

find their way, to feel se - cure, from lives of tur - bu -
greed - y sys-tems call the tune; for strength to keep our
grind - ing need at af-fluence stare, with tears and thirst for
struc-tures creak and doc-trines swirl, by faith, and in the

lence and rush we come, to seek your peace, our
val - ues straight we come, with trust in you, O
truth and right we come, with long - ing in our
strength of Christ, we strive, in true com - mu - ni -

God, your word to hear, our faith to live.
God, your word to hear, our faith to live.
hearts, your word to hear, our faith to live.
ty, your word to hear, our faith to live.

WORDS: David Sparks
MUSIC: Hal H. Hopson

THUNDER BAY
88.888

2184

Sent Out in Jesus' Name
(Enviado Soy de Dios)

Sent out in Je-sus' name, our hands are rea-dy now to
En - via-do soy de Dios, mi ma - no lis-ta es - tá pa-ra

make the earth the place in which the king-dom comes.
cons - tru - ir con El un mun - do fra - ter - nal.

The an-gels can-not change a world of hurt and pain in -
Los án - ge - les no son en - via-dos a cam - biar un

to a world of love, of jus-tice and of peace. The
mun-do de do - lor por un mun-do de paz. Me

task is ours to do, to set it real-ly free. O
ha to - ca-do a mí ha - cer-lo rea - li - dad; a -

help us to o - bey and car-ry out your will.
yú - da - me, Se - ñor, a ha - cer tu vo-lun - tad.

WORDS: Anon.; trans. by Jorge Maldonado, alt.
MUSIC: Trad. Cuban; arr. by Carmen Peña

ENVIADO
12 12.12 12 D

2185

For One Great Peace

1. This thread I weave, this step I dance, this
2. this pot I shape, this fire I light, this
3. this check I write, this march I join, this

WORDS: Shirley Erena Murray
MUSIC: Jim Strathdee

POXON
LM

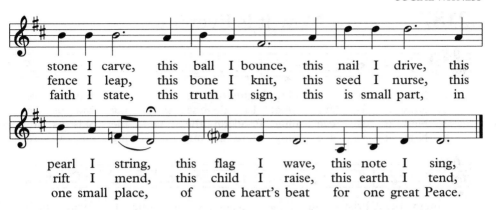

stone I carve, this ball I bounce, this nail I drive, this
fence I leap, this bone I knit, this seed I nurse, this
faith I state, this truth I sign, this is small part, in

pearl I string, this flag I wave, this note I sing,
rift I mend, this child I raise, this earth I tend,
one small place, of one heart's beat for one great Peace.

For the Faithful Who Have Answered 2186

1. For the faith-ful who have an-swered when they heard your
2. Man-y eyes have glimpsed the prom-ise, man-y hearts have
3. For this cloud of faith-ful wit-ness, for the com-mon

call to serve, for the man-y ways you led them, test-ing
yearned to see. Man-y ears have heard you call-ing us to
life we share, for the work of peace and jus-tice, for the

will and stretch-ing nerve, for their work and for their wit-ness
great-er lib-er-ty. Some have fall-en in the strug-gle,
gos-pel that we bear, for the vis-ion that our home-land

as they strove a-gainst the odds, for their cour-age and
oth-ers still are fight-ing on. You are not a-shamed
is your love— deep, high, and broad— for the dif-ferent roads

o-be-dience we give thanks and praise, O God.
to own us. We give thanks and praise, O God.
we trav-el we give thanks and praise, O God.

WORDS: Sylvia G. Dunstan
MUSIC: *Trier Gesangbuch*
Words © 1991 GIA Publications, Inc.

OMNI DIE
87.87 D

2187   Now It Is Evening

1. Now it is eve - ning: Lights of the cit - y bid us re -
2. Now it is eve - ning: Lit - tle ones sleep - ing bid us re -
3. Now it is eve - ning: Food on the ta - ble bids us re -
4. Now it is eve - ning: Here in our meet - ing may we re -

mem - ber Christ is our light. Man - y are lone - ly, who will be
mem - ber Christ is our peace. Some are ne - glect - ed, who will be
mem - ber Christ is our life. Man - y are hun - gry, who will be
mem - ber Christ is our friend. Some may be strang - ers, who will be

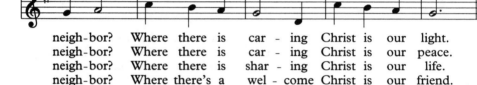

neigh - bor? Where there is car - ing Christ is our light.
neigh - bor? Where there is car - ing Christ is our peace.
neigh - bor? Where there is shar - ing Christ is our life.
neigh - bor? Where there's a wel - come Christ is our friend.

WORDS: Fred Pratt Green (John 8:12; 14:6, 27; 15:15)   EVENING HYMN
MUSIC: David Haas   55.54 D

2188   The Family Prayer Song

1. Come and fill our homes with your pres - ence;
2. Lord we vow to live ho - ly,

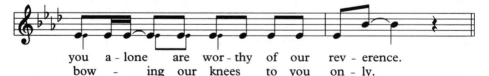

you a - lone are wor - thy of our rev - erence.
bow - ing our knees to you on - ly.

Refrain

As for me and my house, we will serve the Lord. As for

WORDS: Morris Chapman (Josh. 24:15)   FAMILY PRAYER
MUSIC: Morris Chapman   Irregular with Refrain

me and my house, we will serve the Lord. As for me and my house,

we will serve the Lord.   We   will serve   the Lord.

A Mother Lined a Basket   2189

1. A moth-er lined a   bas-ket   to   keep her ba - by   dry,
2. A moth-er sewed a   jack-et   lined   in   the soft - est   wool,
3. A moth-er laid her   ba - by   in   man-ger lined with straw;
4. Like Joch - e - bed and Han-nah,   and   Ma - ry, too, we know

then rocked him   on   a   riv - er,   lest   he   a - wake and   cry.
then dressed her   lit - tle   boy-child,   her   cup   of   bless-ing   full.
then,   in   the   shep-herd's sto - ry,   his   call from God fore - saw.
the   hard - est   part   of   lov - ing   is   learn-ing   to   let   go.

She   let   a   prin-cess name him   her   son that   he might live.
She brought him   to   the   tem - ple where he would serve and   live.
She   nur - tured him and taught him   the way that   he must live.
So   when   we   send our   chil - dren out   in   the   world to   live,

God's peo-ple   had   a   lead - er.   She   had such hope   to   give.
God's peo-ple   had   a   proph - et.   She   had such faith   to   give.
God's peo-ple   had   a   sav - ior.   She   had such love   to   give.
grant   us such hope and   faith, God,   and   love   e - nough to   give.

WORDS: Mary Nelson Keithahn (Exod. 2:1-10; 6:20; 1 Sam. 1; Luke 2)   WEST MAIN
MUSIC: John D. Horman   76.76 D

2190   Bring Forth the Kingdom

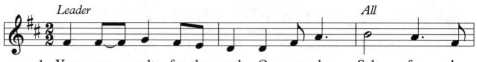

Leader   *All*

1. You are salt for the earth, O peo-ple: Salt for the
2. You are a light on the hill, O peo-ple: Light for the
3. You are a seed of the Word, O peo-ple: Bring forth the
4. We are a blest and a pil-grim peo-ple: Bound for the

Leader

King-dom of God! Share the fla-vor of
Cit-y of God! Shine so ho-ly and
King-dom of God! Seeds of mer-cy and
King-dom of God! Love our jour-ney and

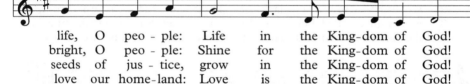

All

life, O peo-ple: Life in the King-dom of God!
bright, O peo-ple: Shine for the King-dom of God!
seeds of jus-tice, grow in the King-dom of God!
love our home-land: Love is the King-dom of God!

Refrain

Bring forth the King-dom of mer-cy, bring forth the

King-dom of peace; bring forth the King-dom of jus-tice,

bring forth the Cit-y of God! _____

WORDS: Marty Haugen (Matt. 5:13-16)   BRING FORTH THE KINGDOM
MUSIC: Marty Haugen   Irregular with Refrain

© 1986 GIA Publications, Inc.

SOCIAL WITNESS, *see further:*

2232   Come Now, O Prince of Peace ("O-So-So")
2134   Forgive Us, Lord ("Perdón, Señor")
2240   One God and Father of Us All
2222   The Servant Song

Bless Now, O God, the Journey 2191

1. Bless now, O God, the jour-ney that all your peo-ple make,
2. Bless so-journ-ers and pil-grims who share this wind-ing way,
3. Di-vine E-ter-nal Lov-er, you meet us on the road.

the path through noise and si-lence, the way of give and take.
whose hope burns through the ter-rors, whose love sus-tains the day.
We wait for lands of prom-ise where milk and hon-ey flow.

The trail is found in des-ert and winds the moun-tain 'round,
We yearn for ho-ly free-dom while oft-en we are bound.
But wait-ing not for plac-es, you meet us all a-round.

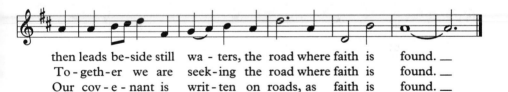

then leads be-side still wa-ters, the road where faith is found. __
To-geth-er we are seek-ing the road where faith is found. __
Our cov-e-nant is writ-ten on roads, as faith is found. __

WORDS: Sylvia G. Dunstan
MUSIC: Basil Harwood

THORNBURY
76.76 D

Words © 1991 GIA Publications, Inc.

2192

Freedom Is Coming

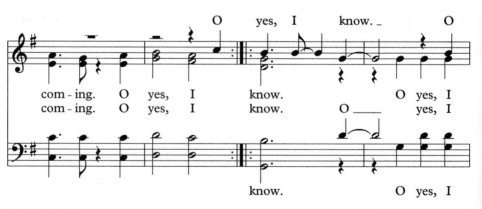

WORDS: Trad. South African
MUSIC: Trad. South African

FREEDOM IS COMING
Irregular

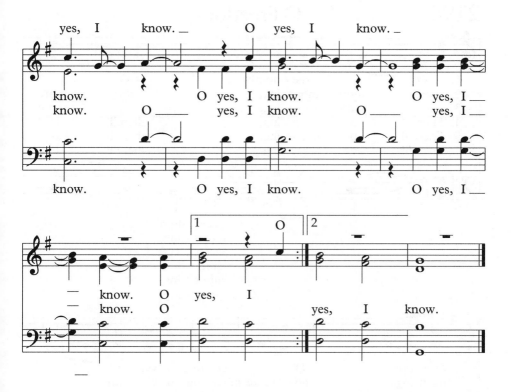

yes, I know. _ O yes, I know. _

know. O yes, I know. O yes, I _
know. O _ yes, I know. O _ yes, I _

know. O yes, I know. O yes, I _

know. O yes, I know. O yes, I _

know. O yes, I
know. O yes, I know.

Lord, Listen to Your Children Praying 2193

Lord, lis-ten to your chil-dren pray - ing, _____

Lord, send your Spir-it in this place; _____

Lord, lis-ten to your chil-dren pray - ing, _____ send us

love, send us power, send us grace. _____

WORDS: Ken Medema
MUSIC: Ken Medema
© 1973 Hope Publishing Co.

CHILDREN PRAYING
98.99

2194

O Freedom

1. O free - dom! O
2. No more moan-ing, no more
3. No more weep-ing, no more
4. There'll be sing - ing, there'll be
5. There'll be shout-ing, there'll be
6. There'll be pray - ing, there'll be

free - dom!
moan - ing,
weep - ing,
sing - ing,
shout - ing,
pray - ing,

free - dom! O free-dom o - ver me.
moan-ing, no more moan-ing o - ver me.
weep-ing, no more weep-ing o - ver me.
sing - ing, there'll be sing - ing o - ver me.
shout-ing, there'll be shout-ing o - ver me.
pray - ing, there'll be pray-ing o - ver me.

free-dom!
moan-ing,
weep-ing,
sing - ing,
shout-ing,
pray - ing,

Refrain

And be - fore I'll be a slave, I'd be

WORDS: African American spiritual
MUSIC: African American spiritual; arr. by John Bell

O FREEDOM
Irregular with Refrain

buried in my grave, and go home to my

Lord and be free. (O freedom.) free.

1-5 6

In the Lord I'll Be Ever Thankful 2195

In the Lord I'll be ev-er thank-ful, in the Lord I will re-

joice! Look to God, do not be a-fraid. Lift up your

voic-es, the Lord is near, lift up your voic-es, the Lord is near.

WORDS: Jacques Berthier
MUSIC: Jacques Berthier

ITLIBET
Irregular

2196   We Walk by Faith

1., 5. We walk by faith, and not by sight: No
2. We may not touch his hands and side, nor
3. Help then, O Lord, our un - be - lief, and
4. That when our life of faith is done in

gra - cious words we hear _____ of him who spoke as
fol - low where he trod; _____ yet in his prom - ise
may our faith a - bound; ___ to call on you when
realms of clear - er light _____ we may be - hold you

none e'er spoke, but we be - lieve him near. _____
we re - joice, and cry, "My Lord and God!" ___
you are near, and seek where you are found: ___
as you are in full and end - less sight. ___

WORDS: Henry Alford, alt. (Mark 9:24; John 20:27-29)   MARTYRDOM
MUSIC: Attr. to Hugh Wilson   CM

2197   Lord of All Hopefulness

1. Lord of all hope - ful - ness, Lord of all joy, whose
2. Lord of all ea - ger - ness, Lord of all faith, whose
3. Lord of all kind - li - ness, Lord of all grace, your
4. Lord of all gen - tle - ness, Lord of all calm, whose

WORDS: Jan Struther   SLANE
MUSIC: Irish folk melody   10 11.11 12

trust, ev - er child - like, no cares could de - stroy: Be
strong hands were skilled at the plane and the lathe: Be
hands swift to wel - come, your arms to em - brace: Be
voice is con - tent - ment, whose pres - ence is balm: Be

there at our wak - ing, and give us, we pray, your
there at our la - bors, and give us, we pray, your
there at our hom - ing, and give us, we pray, your
there at our sleep - ing, and give us, we pray, your

bliss in our hearts, Lord, at the break of the day.
strength in our hearts, Lord, at the noon of the day.
love in our hearts, Lord, at the eve of the day.
peace in our hearts, Lord, at the end of the day.

Stay with Me   2198
(Noho Pū)

Stay with me, re - main here with me, watch and
No - ho pū no - ho mai me ia'u ki - a'i a

pray, watch and pray.
pu - le kiai a pule.

WORDS: Jacques Berthier; Hawaiian trans.
      by Malcolm Naea Chun (Matt. 26:41; Mark 14:38)
MUSIC: Jacques Berthier

STAY WITH ME
Irregular

2199

Stay with Us

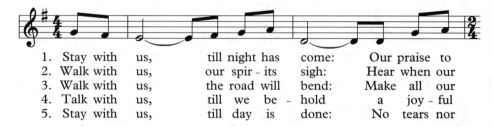

1. Stay with us, till night has come: Our praise to
2. Walk with us, our spir-its sigh: Hear when our
3. Walk with us, the road will bend: Make all our
4. Talk with us, till we be-hold a joy-ful
5. Stay with us, till day is done: No tears nor

you this day be sung. Bless our bread, o-pen our
wea-ry spir-its cry, feel a-gain our loss, our
weep-ing, wail-ing end. Wipe our tears, for-give our
life you will un-fold: Heal our eyes to see the
dark shall dim the sun. Cheer the heart, your grace im-

eyes: Je-sus, be our great sur-prise.
pain: Je-sus, take us to your side.
fears: Je-sus, lift the heav-y cross.
prize: Je-sus, take us to the light.
part: Je-sus, bring e-ter-nal life.

WORDS: Herbert F. Brokering (Luke 24:13-35)
MUSIC: Walter L. Pelz

STAY WITH US
78.77

© 1980 Concordia Publishing House

2200

O Lord, Hear My Prayer

O Lord, hear my prayer. O Lord, hear my prayer.

WORDS: Jacques Berthier (Ps. 102:1-2)
MUSIC: Jacques Berthier

HEAR MY PRAYER
Irregular

© 1984 Les Presses de Taizé (France). Used by permission of GIA Publications, Inc.

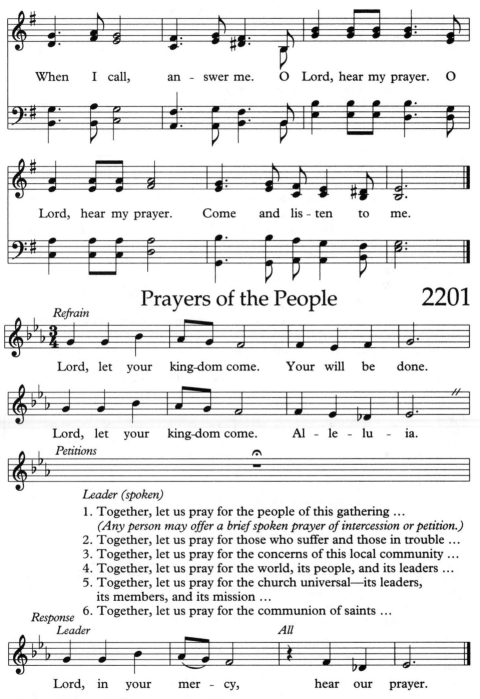

When I call, an - swer me. O Lord, hear my prayer. O

Lord, hear my prayer. Come and lis - ten to me.

Prayers of the People 2201

Refrain

Lord, let your king-dom come. Your will be done.

Lord, let your king-dom come. Al - le - lu - ia.

Petitions

Leader (spoken)

1. Together, let us pray for the people of this gathering ...
   (Any person may offer a brief spoken prayer of intercession or petition.)
2. Together, let us pray for those who suffer and those in trouble ...
3. Together, let us pray for the concerns of this local community ...
4. Together, let us pray for the world, its people, and its leaders ...
5. Together, let us pray for the church universal—its leaders,
   its members, and its mission ...
6. Together, let us pray for the communion of saints ...

Response

Leader   *All*

Lord, in your mer - cy, hear our prayer.

WORDS: From *The United Methodist Hymnal* (Matt. 6:10)
MUSIC: Bonnie Johansen-Werner

2202 Come Away with Me

1. Come a - way with me to a qui - et
2. Come and pray with me on a gen - tle
3. Come to - day with thoughts of the count - less
4. Come and say, in words whis - pered from your
5. Come a - way with me to a qui - et

place, a - part from the world with its fran - tic
sea, on top of a hill in the Gal - i -
ways that God's stead - fast love bless - es all our
soul, the feel - ings and ac - tions you can't con -
place, to God's lov - ing arms wait - ing to em -

pace, to pray, re - flect, and seek God's grace.
lee, in gar - dens like Geth - se - ma - ne.
days, and join with me in si - lent praise.
trol. Your spir - it needs to be made whole.
brace all those who come in hope of grace.

Come a - way with me. Come a - way.

WORDS: Mary Nelson Keithahn
MUSIC: John D. Horman

RECREATION
10 10.88

© 1997 Abingdon Press (admin. by The Copyright Co., Nashville, TN)

2203 In His Time

1. In his time, _____ in his time; _____ he makes
2. In your time, _____ in your time; _____ you make

all things beau - ti - ful in his time. _____ Lord, please
all things beau - ti - ful in your time. _____ Lord, my

WORDS: Diane Ball (Eccles. 3:11)
MUSIC: Diane Ball

GOD'S TIME
Irregular

© 1978 CCCM Music (admin. by Maranatha! Music c/o The Copyright Co., Nashville, TN)

show me ev-ery day as you're teach-ing me your way, that you
life to you I bring; may each song I have to sing be to

do just what you say in your time. _____
you a love-ly thing in your time. _____

Morning, Evening   2204

Morn-ing break-ing, song-bird in the sky sings a lul-la-by to the

night. And I find that I am wak-ing to the ris-ing sun.

I sing to the One who is the Light. I sing to the God who made the day, the

God who guides my way; the God who'll al-ways say, "I'm right be-side you."

So morn-ing, eve-ning, all day long I sing a song to the God of

morn-ing. _____ To the God of ___ to the Lord of love. ___

WORDS: Steve Swayne (2 Cor. 4:6, 16b)
MUSIC: Steve Swayne
© 1988 Fred Bock Music Co., Inc.

MORNING, EVENING
Irregular

GRACE

2205   The Fragrance of Christ

Refrain

Lord, may our prayer rise like in-cense in your sight, may this place be filled with the fra-grance of Christ. _____

1. I will thank you, Lord, with all of my heart, you have heard the words of my mouth. _____ In the pres-ence of the Lord I will bless you, _____ I will a - dore be-fore your ho - ly tem - ple. _____

2. I will thank you, Lord, for your faith - ful-ness and love, be - yond all my hopes and dreams. _____ On the day that I called you an - swered; _____ you gave life to the strength of my soul. _____

3. All who live on earth shall give you thanks when they hear the words of your voice. _____ And all shall sing of your ways: _____ "How great is the glo - ry of God!" _____

Fine

D.C.

WORDS: David Haas (Ps. 138:1-5; 141:2)   INCENSE
MUSIC: David Haas   Irregular with Refrain

© 1989 GIA Publications, Inc.

Without Seeing You

2206

Refrain

With-out see-ing you, we love you; with-out

touch-ing you, we em-brace; with-out know-ing you, we

Fine

fol-low; with-out see-ing you, _____ we be-lieve. _____

1. We re - turn to you deep with - in, leave the
2. The spar - row will find a home, near to
3. For - ev - er we sing to you of your
4. For you are our shep - herd, there is

past to the dust; turn to you with tears and
you, O God; how hap - py, we who
good - ness, O God; pro - claim - ing to
noth - ing that we need; in green pas - tures we will

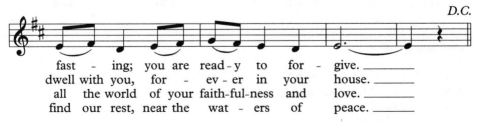

D.C.

fast - ing; you are read-y to for - give. _____
dwell with you, for - ev - er in your house. _____
all the world of your faith-ful-ness and love. _____
find our rest, near the wat - ers of peace. _____

WORDS: David Haas (Ps. 23:1-2; 1 Pet. 1:8)
MUSIC: David Haas

WE BELIEVE
Irregular with Refrain

© 1993 GIA Publications, Inc.

2207 Lord, Listen to Your Children

On bend-ed knee with need-y hearts we come and pray. Lord, lis-ten to your chil - dren. With will-ing hearts and o-pen arms we come and pray. Lord, lis - ten to your chil - dren. With sim - ple words of heart-felt thanks we come. Be liev - ing in your prom - is - es, we come. On

Last time to Coda

D.S. al Coda

CODA

chil - dren, lis-ten to your chil - dren.

WORDS: Handt Hanson and Paul Murakami
MUSIC: Handt Hanson and Paul Murakami

LISTEN
Irregular

PRAYER, TRUST, HOPE, *see further:*

2128   Come and Find the Quiet Center
2127   Come and See
2275   Kyrie (Dvořák/Schram)
2277   Lord, Have Mercy

Christ the Victorious

1. Christ the vic - tor - i - ous, give to your ser - vants
2. On - ly im - mor - tal one, might - y Cre - a - tor!
3. God - spo - ken pro - phe - cy, word at cre - a - tion:
4. Christ the vic - tor - i - ous, give to your ser - vants

rest with your saints in the re - gions of light.
We are your crea - tures and child - ren of earth.
"You came from dust and to dust shall re - turn."
rest with your saints in the re - gions of light.

Grief and pain end - ed, and sigh - ing no long - er,
From earth you formed us, both glor - i - ous and mor - tal,
Yet at the grave shall we raise up our glad song,
Grief and pain end - ed, and sigh - ing no long - er,

there may they find ev - er - last - ing life.
and to the earth shall we all re - turn.
"Al - le - lu - ia, al - le - lu - ia!"
there may they find ev - er - last - ing life.

WORDS: Carl P. Daw Jr. (Rev. 21:4)
MUSIC: Alexis Feodorovich Lvov

RUSSIAN ANTHEM
11 10.11 9

2209

How Long, O Lord

1. How long, O Lord,   will you for - get
2. How long, O Lord,   will you for - sake
3. How long, O Lord?   But you for - give

an an - swer to my prayer?
and leave me in this way?
with mer - cy from a - bove.

No to - kens of your love I see, your face is turned a -
When will you come to my re - lief? My heart is o - ver -
I find that all your ways are just; I learn to praise you

way from me; I wres - tle with de - spair!
whelmed with grief, by e - vil night and day!
and to trust in your un - fail - ing love!

WORDS: Barbara Woollett (Ps. 13)
MUSIC: Christopher Norton

HOW LONG
86.886

Words © 1990 Jubilate Hymns (admin. by Hope Publishing Co.); music © 1993 Harper
   Collins Religious (admin. by The Copyright Co., Nashville, TN)

2210

Joy Comes with the Dawn

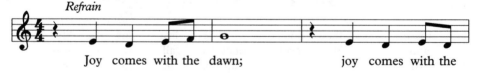

Refrain

Joy comes with the dawn; joy comes with the

morn - ing sun; joy springs from the tomb and

WORDS: Gordon Light (Ps. 30:5)
MUSIC: Gordon Light

DAWN
4.77 with Refrain

© 1985 The Common Cup Co.

Fine

scat-ters the night with her song, joy comes with the dawn.

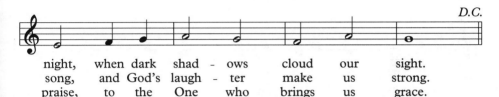

1. Weep-ing may come; weep-ing may come in the
2. Sor - row will turn, sor - row will turn in - to
3. We will re - joice, we will re - joice, and give

D.C.

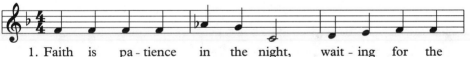

night, when dark shad - ows cloud our sight.
song, and God's laugh - ter make us strong.
praise, to the One who brings us grace.

Faith Is Patience in the Night   2211

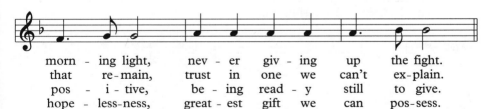

1. Faith is pa - tience in the night, wait - ing for the
2. Faith is laugh - ter in our pain, joy in plea - sures
3. Faith is stead - fast will to live, stand - ing firm and
4. Faith is cour - age un - der stress, con - fi - dence in

morn - ing light, nev - er giv - ing up the fight.
that re - main, trust in one we can't ex - plain.
pos - i - tive, be - ing read - y still to give.
hope - less-ness, great - est gift we can pos - sess.

|1-3| |4|

Spir - it God give us faith. give us faith.

WORDS: Mary Nelson Keithahn
MUSIC: John D. Horman

FAITHSONG
77.76

2212

My Life Flows On
(How Can I Keep from Singing)

1. My life flows on in end-less song, a-bove earth's la-men-
2. Through all the tu-mult and the strife, I hear that mu-sic
3. What though my joys and com-forts die? I know my Sav-ior
4. The peace of Christ makes fresh my heart, a foun-tain ev-er

ta-tion. I hear the clear, though far-off hymn that
ring-ing. It finds an ech-o in my soul. How
liv-eth. What though the dark-ness gath-er round? Songs
spring-ing! All things are mine since I am his! How

Refrain

hails a new cre-a-tion.
can I keep from sing-ing?
in the night he giv-eth.   No   storm can shake my
can I keep from sing-ing?

in-most calm   while   to that Rock   I'm   cling-ing. Since

WORDS: Robert Lowry
MUSIC: Robert Lowry

HOW CAN I KEEP FROM SINGING
87.87 with Refrain

love is Lord of heaven and earth, how can I keep from sing-ing?

Healer of Our Every Ill   2213

Refrain

Heal-er of our ev-ery ill, light of each to-mor-row,

Fine

give us peace be-yond our fear, and hope be-yond our sor - row.

1. You who know our fears and sad-ness, grace us with your
2. In the pain and joy be-hold-ing how your grace is
3. Give us strength to love each oth - er, ev - ery sis - ter,
4. You who know each thought and feel - ing, teach us all your

peace and glad - ness; Spir - it of all com - fort,
still un - fold - ing, give us all your vi - sion,
ev - ery broth - er; Spir - it of all kind - ness,
way of heal - ing; Spir - it of com-pas - sion,

D.C.

fill our hearts. _____
God of love. _____
be our guide. _____
fill each heart. _____

WORDS: Marty Haugen
MUSIC: Marty Haugen

HEALER OF OUR EVERY ILL
88.63 with Refrain

© 1987 GIA Publications, Inc.

2214 Lead Me, Guide Me

Lead me, guide me, a-long the way,
for if you lead me, I can-not stray.
Lord, let me walk each day with thee.
Lead me, O Lord, lead me. _____

Stanzas included in other editions.
WORDS: Doris Akers
MUSIC: Doris Akers

LEAD ME, GUIDE ME
Irregular

© 1953 Doris Akers, renewed (admin. by Unichappell Music, Inc.)

2215 Cares Chorus

I cast all my cares up-on you, _____ I
lay all of my bur-dens down at your feet, and
an-y-time that I don't know what to do, I will
cast all my cares up-on you. _____

WORDS: Kelly Willard (Ps. 55:22; 1 Pet. 5:7)
MUSIC: Kelly Willard

CARES CHORUS
Irregular

© 1978 Maranatha Praise, Inc. (admin. by The Copyright Co., Nashville, TN)

When We Are Called to Sing Your Praise 2216

1. When we are called to sing your praise with hearts so filled with pain that we would rather sit and weep or stand up to com-plain, re-mind us, God, you un-der-stand the bur-dens that we bear; you, too, have walked the shad-owed way and known our deep de-spair.

2. When we are called to sing your praise and can-not find our voice, be-cause our los-ses leave us now no rea-son to re-joice, re-mind us, God, that you ac-cept our sad la-ments in prayer; you, too, have walked the shad-owed way and known our deep de-spair.

3. When we are called to sing your praise and life a-head looks grim, still give us faith and hope e-nough to break forth in a hymn, a thank-ful hymn, great God of Love, that you are ev-ery-where; you walk the shad-owed way with us and keep us in your care.

WORDS: Mary Nelson Keithahn
MUSIC: Trad. English melody

KINGSFOLD
CMD

2217   My Help

I lift my eyes to the hills, __ from

where does my help come? It comes from God, who made

heav-en and earth, and the love __ we share from with-in. __

WORDS: Chip Andrus (Ps. 121)
MUSIC: Chip Andrus
© 2000 Chip Andrus

MY HELP
Irregular

2218   You Are Mine

1. __ I will come to you in the si - lence, __
2. __ I am hope for all who are hope-less, __
3. __ I am strength for all the de - spair-ing, __
4. I am the Word that leads all to free - dom, I

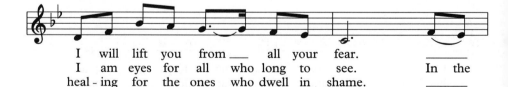

I will lift you from __ all your fear. _____
I am eyes for all who long to see. In the
heal - ing for the ones who dwell in shame. _____
am the peace the world can - not give. _____

WORDS: David Haas (Ps. 46:10; Isa. 43:1; John 14:27)
MUSIC: David Haas
© 1991 GIA Publications, Inc.

YOU ARE MINE
Irregular with Refrain

You will hear my voice, I claim you as my choice, be
shad-ows of the night, I will be your light,
All the blind will see, the lame will all run free, and
I will call your name, em - brac-ing all your pain, stand

still and know I am here. _____
come and rest in
all will know my
up, now walk, and

1

me. _____
name. _____
live! _____

2-4

Refrain

Do not be a-fraid, I am

with you. I have called you each by name.

Come and fol-low me, I will bring you home; I

love you and you are mine. _____

2219 Goodness Is Stronger than Evil

WORDS: From *An African Prayer Book*, selected by Desmond Tutu
MUSIC: John Bell

GOODNESS IS STRONGER
Irregular

We Are God's People

1. We are God's peo - ple, the cho - sen of the
2. We are God's loved ones, the Bride of Christ, our
3. We are the bod - y of which the Lord is
4. We are a tem - ple, the Spir - it's dwell - ing

Lord, born of the Spir - it, es -
Lord, for we have known it, the
Head, called to o - bey Christ, now
place, formed in great weak - ness, a

tab - lished by the Word. Our cor - ner - stone is
love of God out - poured. Now let us learn how
ris - en from the dead. God wills us be a
cup to hold God's grace. We die a - lone, for

Christ a - lone, and strong in Christ we stand; O
to re - turn the gift of love once given; O
fam - i - ly di - verse, yet tru - ly one; O
on its own each em - ber los - es fire; yet

let us live trans - par - ent - ly and
let us share each joy and care and
let us give our gifts to God and
joined in one the flame burns on to

walk heart to heart and hand in hand.
live with a zeal that pleas - es heaven.
so shall God's work on earth be done.
give warmth and light and to in - spire.

WORDS: Bryan Jeffery Leech (John 3:5-8; 1 Cor. 3:16; Col. 1:18; 1 Pet. 2:9)
MUSIC: Johannes Brahms, arr. by Fred Bock

SYMPHONY
11 11 13.89

2221 In Unity We Lift Our Song

1. In u-ni-ty we lift our song of grate-ful a-dor-a - tion, for broth-ers brave and sis-ters strong. What cause for cel-e-bra - tion! For those whose faith-ful - ness has kept us through dis-tress, who've shared with us our plight,

2. For sto-ries told and told a-gain to ev-ery gen-er-a - tion, to give us strength in times of pain, to give us con-so-la - tion. Our spir-its to re - vive to keep our dreams a - live, when we are far from home

3. For sa-cred scrip-tures hand-ed down, a bless-ed trust and trea - sure, which give us hope when hope is gone and make us weep with plea - sure. And when our eyes grow blind and death is close be-hind, we shall re-cite them still

4. For God our way, our bread, our rest, of all these gifts the Giv - er. Our strength, our guide, our nur-turing breast whose hand will yet de-liv - er. Who keeps us till the day when night shall pass a - way, when hate and fear are gone

WORDS: Ken Medema

MUSIC: Martin Luther; harm. from *The New Hymnal for American Youth*

EIN' FESTE BURG

87.87.66.667

Words © 1994 Brier Patch Music

who've held us in the night, the bless-ed con-gre-ga - tion.
and e - vil sea - sons come; how firm is our foun-da - tion.
whose words our hearts can fill with hope be-yond all mea - sure.
and all our work is done, and we shall sing for - ev - er.

The Servant Song 2222

1., 6. Broth- er, sis - ter, let me serve you, let me be as
2. We are pil - grims on a jour-ney; we're to - geth - er
3. I will hold the Christ-light for you in the night-time
4. I will weep when you are weep-ing; when you laugh, I'll
5. When we sing to God in heav - en, we shall find such

Christ to you; pray that I may have the grace to
on this road. We are here to help each oth - er
of your fear; I will hold my hand out to you,
laugh with you. I will share your joy and sor - row
har - mo - ny, born of all we've known to - geth - er

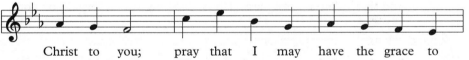

let you be my ser - vant, too.
walk the mile and bear the load.
speak the peace you long to hear.
till we've seen this jour - ney through.
of Christ's love and ag - o - ny.

WORDS: Richard Gillard (Matt. 20:26) THE SERVANT SONG
MUSIC: Richard Gillard 87.87

2223 They'll Know We Are Christians by Our Love

1. We are one in the Spir-it, we are one in the Lord,
2. We will walk with each oth-er, we will walk hand in hand,
3. We will work with each oth-er, we will work side by side,
4. All praise to the Fa-ther, from whom all things come,

we are one in the Spir-it, we are one in the Lord,
we will walk with each oth-er, we will walk hand in hand,
we will work with each oth-er, we will work side by side,
and all praise to Christ Je-sus, God's on-ly Son,

and we pray that all u-ni-ty may one day be re-stored:
and to-geth-er we'll spread the news that God is in our land:
and we'll guard hu-man dig-ni-ty and save hu-man pride:
and all praise to the Spir-it, who makes us one:

Refrain

And they'll know we are Chris-tians by our love, by our

love; yes, they'll know we are Chris-tians by our love. _____

WORDS: Peter Scholtes (John 13:34-35; Eph. 4:4-6)
MUSIC: Peter Scholtes

ST. BRENDAN'S
76.76.86 with Refrain

© 1966 F.E.L. Publications, assigned 1991 to The Lorenz Corp.

2224 Make Us One

Make us one, Lord, make us one; Ho-ly

WORDS: Carol Cymbala (John 17:22-23)
MUSIC: Carol Cymbala

MAKE US ONE
Irregular

© 1991 Word Music, Inc. and Carol Joy Music (admin. by Integrated Copyright Group)

Spir - it, make us one. Let your love flow so the

world will know we are one in you.

Who Is My Mother, Who Is My Brother? 2225

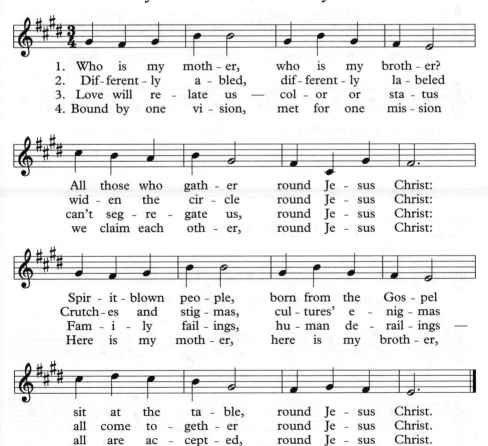

1. Who is my moth - er, who is my broth - er?
2. Dif - ferent - ly a - bled, dif - ferent - ly la - beled
3. Love will re - late us — col - or or sta - tus
4. Bound by one vi - sion, met for one mis - sion

All those who gath - er round Je - sus Christ:
wid - en the cir - cle round Je - sus Christ:
can't seg - re - gate us, round Je - sus Christ:
we claim each oth - er, round Je - sus Christ:

Spir - it - blown peo - ple, born from the Gos - pel
Crutch - es and stig - mas, cul - tures' e - nig - mas
Fam - i - ly fail - ings, hu - man de - rail - ings —
Here is my moth - er, here is my broth - er,

sit at the ta - ble, round Je - sus Christ.
all come to - geth - er round Je - sus Christ.
all are ac - cept - ed, round Je - sus Christ.
kin - dred in Spir - it, through Je - sus Christ.

WORDS: Shirley Erena Murray (Matt. 12:46-50; Mark 3:31-35; Luke 8:19-21)
MUSIC: Jack Schrader

KINDRED
54.54 D

2226   Bind Us Together

Bind us to-geth-er, Lord, bind us to-geth-er with cords that

can-not be bro - ken. Bind us to-geth-er, Lord,

Fine

bind us to-geth-er, Lord, bind us to-geth-er in love. ____

There is on-ly one God, ____ there is on-ly one King; ____

D.C. al Fine

There is on-ly one bod-y, _____ that is why we sing. ____

WORDS: Bob Gillman (Col. 3:14)
MUSIC: Bob Gillman
© 1977 ThankYou Music

BIND US TOGETHER
Irregular

2227   We Are the Body of Christ

One heart, one Spir - it, one voice to

praise you, we are the bod - y of Christ.

One goal, one vi - sion: To see you ex -

WORDS: Scott Wesley Brown and David Hampton (1 Cor. 12)
MUSIC: Scott Wesley Brown and David Hampton
© 1998 New Spring Publishing, Inc. (a div. of Brentwood-Benson Music Publishing, Inc.)/SongWard Music.

BODY OF CHRIST
Irregular

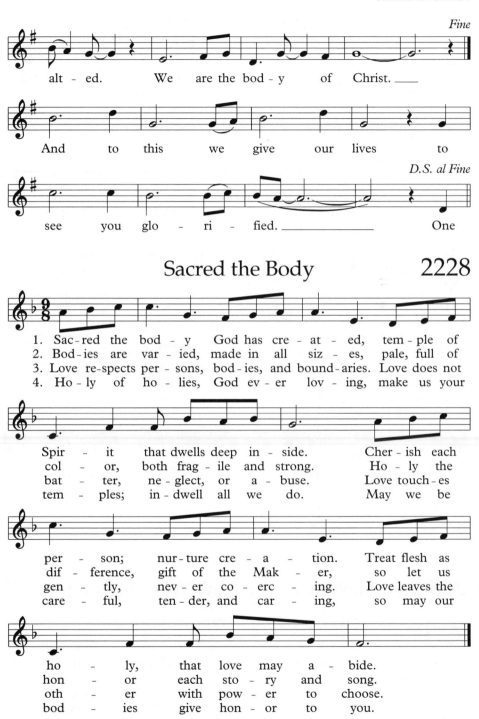

Fine

alt - ed. We are the bod - y of Christ. ___

And to this we give our lives to

D.S. al Fine

see you glo - ri - fied. _____ One

Sacred the Body 2228

1. Sac-red the bod - y God has cre - at - ed, tem - ple of
2. Bod-ies are var - ied, made in all siz - es, pale, full of
3. Love re-spects per - sons, bod-ies, and bound-aries. Love does not
4. Ho - ly of ho - lies, God ev - er lov - ing, make us your

Spir - it that dwells deep in - side. Cher - ish each
col - or, both frag - ile and strong. Ho - ly the
bat - ter, ne - glect, or a - buse. Love touch-es
tem - ples; in - dwell all we do. May we be

per - son; nur - ture cre - a - tion. Treat flesh as
dif - ference, gift of the Mak - er, so let us
gen - tly, nev - er co - erc - ing. Love leaves the
care - ful, ten - der, and car - ing, so may our

ho - ly, that love may a - bide.
hon - or each sto - ry and song.
oth - er with pow - er to choose.
bod - ies give hon - or to you.

WORDS: Ruth Duck (1 Cor. 3:16; 13:4-7)
MUSIC: W. Daniel Landes

RUDDLE
10 10.10 10

2229   We Are One in Christ Jesus
(Somos Uno en Cristo)

We are one in Christ Je-sus, all one bod-y, all one
So-mos u - no en Cris-to, so-mos u - no, so-mos

spir-it, all to-geth-er. We are geth-er. We share one
u - no, u-no só - lo. So-mos só - lo. Un so - lo

God, one might-y Lord, one a-bid-ing
Dios, un so-lo Se - ñor, u-na so - la

faith, one bind-ing love, one sin-gle bap - ti - sm, one Ho-ly
fe, un so-lo a - mor, un so-lo bau-tis - mo, un so-lo Es-

Com-fort-er, the Ho-ly Spir - it, u - nit-ing all.
pí - ri - tu y e - se es el Con-so-la - dor.

WORDS: Anon.; English trans. by Alice Parker (Eph. 4:4-6)
MUSIC: Anon.
Trans. © 1996 Abingdon Press (admin. by The Copyright Co., Nashville, TN)

SOMOS UNO
Irregular

2230   Lord, We Come to Ask Your Blessing

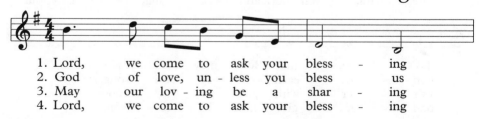

1. Lord, we come to ask your bless - ing
2. God of love, un - less you bless us
3. May our lov - ing be a shar - ing
4. Lord, we come to ask your bless - ing

WORDS: Fred Pratt Green
MUSIC: W. Daniel Landes
Words © 1989 Hope Publishing Co.; music © 1997 Abingdon Press (admin. by The Copyright Co., Nashville, TN)

SUGAR GROVE
87.87

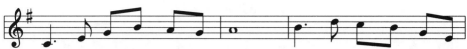

on   the love that makes us   one;   here,   as Chris-tians, to ac -
how can we each oth - er bless?   On - ly   as   you live with-
of   the gifts we each pos - sess;   may   no fail - ure of for-
in   the pres-ence of our friends: Grant us joy that bless-es

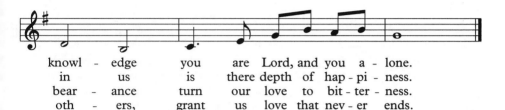

knowl - edge   you   are Lord, and you a - lone.
in   us   is   there depth of hap - pi - ness.
bear - ance   turn our love to bit - ter - ness.
oth - ers,   grant us love that nev - er   ends.

O Look and Wonder 2231
(¡Miren Qué Bueno!)

Refrain   *Last time: Fine*

O   look and won - der,   how   good it   is!
¡Mi - ren qué bue - no,   qué bue - no   es!

1., 2., 3. Look at how good it   is for us to   be here all to - geth - er,
1. *Mi-ren qué bue-no_es cuan-do los her - ma-nos es-tán jun - tos,*
2. *Mi-ren qué bue-no_es cuan-do las her - ma-nas es-tán jun - tas,*
3. *Mi-ren qué bue-no_es cuan-do nos reu - ni-mos to-dos jun - tos,*

D.C.

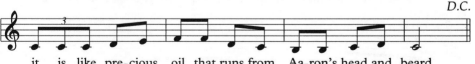

it is like pre-cious oil that runs from Aa-ron's head and beard.
it is like He-bron's dew that falls up - on the hills of Zion.
it is the prom-ise of the Lord e - ter-nal-ly to bless.
es   co-mo_a-cei - te   bue-no de - rra - ma - do so-bre Aa-rón.
se   pa - re-ce_al ro - cí - o   so-bre los mon - tes de Sion.
por-que_el Se - ñor ahí man-da vi - da_e - ter-na_y ben - di - ción.

WORDS: Pablo Sosa; English trans. by George Lockwood (Ps. 133)
MUSIC: Pablo Sosa

MIREN QUÉ BUENO
Irregular with Refrain

2232 Come Now, O Prince of Peace
(O-So-So)

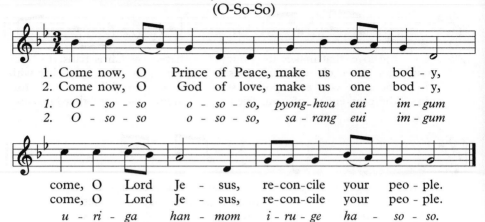

1. Come now, O Prince of Peace, make us one bod-y,
2. Come now, O God of love, make us one bod-y,

1. *O - so - so   o - so - so,   pyong-hwa   eui   im - gum*
2. *O - so - so   o - so - so,   sa - rang   eui   im - gum*

come, O Lord Je - sus, re-con-cile your peo - ple.
come, O Lord Je - sus, re-con-cile your peo - ple.

u - ri - ga   han - mom   i - ru - ge   ha - so - so.
u - ri - ga   han - mom   i - ru - ge   ha - so - so.

3. Come now and set us free,
O God our Savior,
come, O Lord Jesus,
reconcile all nations.

3. *O-so-so o-so-so,*
cha-yu eui im-gum,
u-ri-ga han-mom
i-ru-ge ha-so-so.

4. Come, Hope of unity,
make us one body,
come, O Lord Jesus,
reconcile all nations.

4. *O-so-so o-so-so*
tong-il eui im-gum,
u-ri-ga han-mom
i-ru-ge ha-so-so.

WORDS: Geonyong Lee; English paraphrase by Marion Pope (Isa. 9:6; John 17:22-23)
MUSIC: Geonyong Lee
GEONYONG
65.56

2233 Where Children Belong

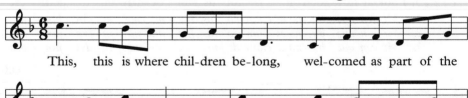

This, this is where chil-dren be-long, wel-comed as part of the

wor - ship - ing throng. Wa - ter, God's Word, bread and

cup, prayer, and song: This is where chil-dren be - long.

WORDS: James Ritchie
MUSIC: James Ritchie
RITCHIE
Irregular

Lead On, O Cloud of Presence 2234

1. Lead on, O cloud of Pres - ence, the ex - o - dus is come,
2. Lead on, O fier - y Pil - lar, we fol - low yet with fears,
3. Lead on, O God of free - dom, and guide us on our way,

1. in wil - der - ness and des - ert our tribe shall make its home.
2. but we shall come re - joic - ing though joy be born of tears.
3. and help us trust the prom - ise through strug - gle and de - lay.

1. Our slav - ery left be - hind us, new hopes with - in us grow.
2. We are not lost, though wan - der - ing, for by your light we come,
3. We pray our sons and daugh - ters may jour - ney to that land

1. We seek the land of prom - ise where milk and hon - ey flow.
2. and we are still God's peo - ple. The jour - ney is our home.
3. where jus - tice dwells with mer - cy, and love is law's de - mand.

WORDS: Ruth Duck (Exod. 13:21-22)
MUSIC: Henry T. Smart

LANCASHIRE
76.76 D

2235-a

We Are Singing
(Siyahamba/Caminando)

Refrain (may be sung in unison throughout)

(English) We are sing - ing* for the
(Zulu) See yah hahm buh koo kah
(Spanish) Ca - mi - nan - do en la

1

Lord is our light, we are sing-ing for the Lord is our light. _
nigh nee kwen kohs. See yah hahm buh koo kah nigh nee kwen kohs. _
luz de Dios, ca - mi - nan-do en la luz de Dios. _

2

Lord is our light. _
nigh nee kwen kohs. _
luz de Dios. _

We are sing - ing for the Lord is, for the
See yah hahm buh koo kah nigh nee, koo kah
Ca - mi - nan - do en la luz, en la

Lord is our light. _
nigh nee kwen kohs. _
luz de Dios. _

*marching, walking, ringing, dancing, praying

WORDS: South Africa (20th cent.); trans. and original verses by Hal H. Hopson
MUSIC: Zulu melody; adapt. and original verses by Hal H. Hopson

SIYAHAMBA
Irregular

Words and music © 1994 Hope Publishing Co.

2235-b

We Are Marching
(Siyahamba/Caminando)

(English) We are march - ing* in the
(Zulu) Si - ya - hamb' e - ku - kha -
(Spanish) Ca - mi - nan - do en la

light of God, we are march-ing in the light of God.
nyen' kwen - khos', si - ya - hamb' e - ku - kha-nyen' kwen - khos.
luz de Dios, ca - mi - nan - do en la luz de Dios.

of God
kwen - khos'
de Dios

We are march-ing in the light of, the
Si - ya - hamb' e - ku - kha-nyen' kwen kha -
Ca - mi - nan - do en la luz de, la

*singing, walking, ringing, dancing, praying, etc.

of God
kwen - khos'
de Dios

WORDS: South Africa (20th cent.)
MUSIC: South Africa (20th cent.)

SIYAHAMBA
Irregular

2236 Gather Us In

1. Here in this place new light is stream-ing,
2. We are the young — our lives are a mys-t'ry,
3. Here we will take the wine and the wa-ter,
4. Not in the dark of build-ings con-fin-ing,

now is the dark - ness van-ished a - way,
we are the old — who yearn for your face,
here we will take the bread of new birth,
not in some heav - en, light-years a - way, but

see in this space our fears and our dream-ings,
we have been sung through - out all of his - t'ry,
here you shall call your sons and your daugh-ters,
here in this place the new light is shin - ing,

brought here to you in the light of this day. _____
called to be light to the whole hu-man race. _____
call us a - new to be salt for the earth. _____
now is the King-dom, now is the day. _____

Gath-er us in — the lost and for - sak - en, gath-er us in — the
Gath-er us in — the rich and the haugh-ty, gath-er us in — the
Give us to drink the wine of com - pas - sion, give us to eat the
Gath-er us in and hold us for - ev - er, gath-er us in and

blind and the lame; call to us now, and we shall a - wak-en,
proud and the strong; give us a heart so meek and so low-ly,
bread that is you; nour-ish us well, and teach us to fash-ion
make us your own; gath-er us in — all peo-ples to-geth-er,

WORDS: Marty Haugen (Matt. 5:13)
MUSIC: Marty Haugen

GATHER US IN
Irregular

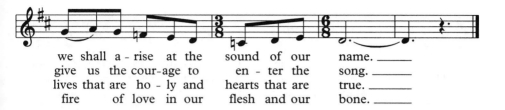

we shall a - rise at the sound of our name. _____
give us the cour-age to en - ter the song. _____
lives that are ho - ly and hearts that are true. _____
fire of love in our flesh and our bone. _____

As a Fire Is Meant for Burning 2237

1. As a fire is meant for burn - ing with a bright and warm-ing
2. We are learn - ers; we are teach - ers; we are pil - grims on the
3. As a green bud in the spring-time is a sign of life re -

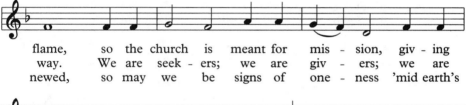

flame, so the church is meant for mis - sion, giv - ing
way. We are seek - ers; we are giv - ers; we are
newed, so may we be signs of one - ness 'mid earth's

glo - ry to God's name. Not to preach our creeds or
ves - sels made of clay. By our gen - tle, lov - ing
peo - ples, man - y hued. As a rain - bow lights the

cus - toms, but to build a bridge of care, we join
ac - tions we would show that Christ is light. In a
heav - ens when a storm is past and gone, may our

hands a - cross the na - tions, find-ing neigh-bors ev - ery-where.
hum - ble, lis-tening Spir - it we would live to God's de - light.
lives re - flect the ra - diance of God's new and glo-rious dawn.

WORDS: Ruth Duck
MUSIC: From *The Sacred Harp*, 1844

BEACH SPRING
87.87 D

2238 In the Midst of New Dimensions

1. In the midst of new di-men-sions, in the face of
2. Through the flood of starv-ing peo-ple, war-ring fac-tions
3. As we stand a world di-vid-ed by our own self-
4. We are man and we are wom-an, all per-sua-sions,
5. Should the threats of dire pre-dic-tions cause us to with-

chang-ing ways, who will lead the pil-grim peo-ples
and de-spair, who will lift the ol-ive branch-es?
seek-ing schemes, grant that we, your glob-al vil-lage,
old and young, each a gift in your cre-a-tion,
draw in pain, may your blaz-ing phoe-nix spir-it

Refrain

wan-dering in their sep-arate ways?
Who will light the flame of care?
might en-vi-sion wid-er dreams. God of rain-bow, fier-y pil-lar,
each a love song to be sung.
res-ur-rect the church a-gain.

lead-ing where the ea-gles soar, we your peo-ple, ours the jour-ney

WORDS: Julian B. Rush (Gen. 9:12-16; Exod. 13:21-22; Num. 14:14)
MUSIC: Julian B. Rush

NEW DIMENSIONS
87.87 with Refrain

© 1994 Julian B. Rush

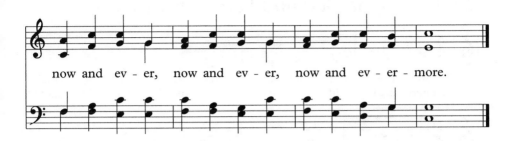

now and ev - er,   now and ev - er,   now and ev - er - more.

Go Ye, Go Ye into the World   2239

Descant
3. Go   ye   now   and

Melody
1.-3. Go   ye,   go   ye   in - to   the   world,   and

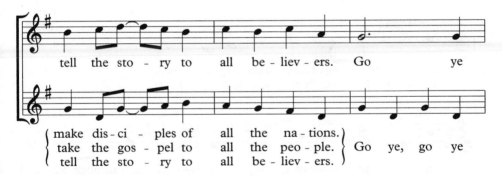

tell   the sto - ry to   all   be - liev - ers.   Go   ye

make dis - ci - ples of   all   the   na - tions.
take the gos - pel to   all   the   peo - ple.   Go   ye,   go   ye
tell   the sto - ry to   all   be - liev - ers.

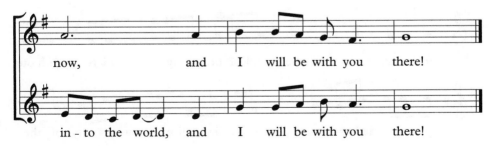

now,   and   I   will be with you   there!

in - to   the   world,   and   I   will be with you   there!

WORDS: Natalie Sleeth (Matt. 28:18-20)   GO YE, GO YE
MUSIC: Natalie Sleeth   8 10.87

2240   One God and Father of Us All

1. All the gifts that God has giv - en by his
(2. There are) dif - ferenc - es a - mong us God can

grace to ev - ery - one were
use to make us strong. Our

meant to give us each a place to serve. _ And if
tap - es - try, his liv - ing work of art. ____ In the

we will come to-geth - er to see his will be done, we will
love that u - ni-fies us by the faith that leads us on, we can

Refrain

share in bless - ings more than we de - serve. There is
fol - low with one pur - pose and one heart.

one God and Fa-ther of us all, a - bove all and through all and

in all. In the bond of ho - ly u - ni-ty with our

spir-its joined as one, let us live lives wor - thy of the

WORDS: Pete Carlson and Kyle Matthews (Eph. 4:6-7)
MUSIC: Pete Carlson and Kyle Matthews

ONE GOD
Irregular with Refrain

call of the one God and Fa-ther of us

1 | **3** *Fine*

all. There are all.

2

all. One bod-y, one peace, one spir-it, one faith, one

D.S.

hope, and to each of us, grace. _____ There is

The Spirit Sends Us Forth to Serve 2241

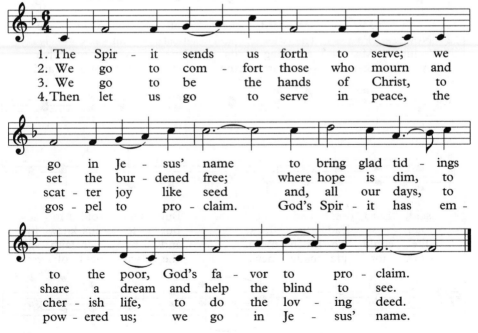

1. The Spir - it sends us forth to serve; we
2. We go to com - fort those who mourn and
3. We go to be the hands of Christ, to
4. Then let us go to serve in peace, the

go in Je - sus' name to bring glad tid - ings
set the bur - dened free; where hope is dim, to
scat - ter joy like seed and, all our days, to
gos - pel to pro - claim. God's Spir - it has em -

to the poor, God's fa - vor to pro - claim.
share a dream and help the blind to see.
cher - ish life, to do the lov - ing deed.
pow - ered us; we go in Je - sus' name.

WORDS: Delores Dufner, OSB
MUSIC: U.S.A. folk melody

LAND OF REST
CM

Words © 1993 Delores Dufner. Published by OCP Publications

2242

Walk with Me

Walk with me, I will walk with you and
build the land that God has planned where love shines through.

1. When Mo - ses heard the call of God he
2. Now Pe - ter was a most un - like - ly
3. Young Ma - ry Mag - da - lene was sure her
4. And when you share your faith with me and

said, "Lord, don't send me." But God told Mo - ses,
man to lead the flock; but Je - sus knew his
life could be much more, and by her faith she
work for life made new, the wit - ness of your

WORDS: John S. Rice (Exod. 3:1–4:20; Matt. 16:13-20; Mark 16:9)
MUSIC: John S. Rice

GLASER
CM with Refrain

© 1988 The Estate of John S. Rice

D.C.

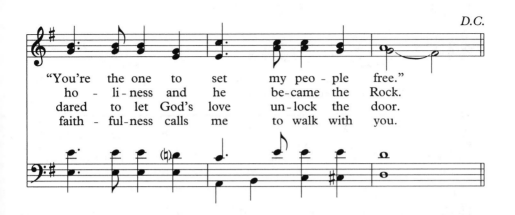

"You're the one to set my peo - ple free."
ho - li - ness and he be-came the Rock.
dared to let God's love un - lock the door.
faith - ful-ness calls me to walk with you.

We All Are One in Mission 2243

1. We all are one in mis - sion; we all are one in call,
2. We all are called for ser - vice, to wit-ness in God's name.
3. Now let us be u - nit - ed, and let our song be heard.

our var-ied gifts u - nit - ed by Christ, the Lord of all.
Our min-is-tries are dif-ferent; our pur - pose is the same:
Now let us be a ves - sel for God's re - deem-ing Word.

A sin - gle great com - mis - sion com - pels us from a - bove
To touch the lives of oth - ers by God's sur-pris-ing grace,
We all are one in mis - sion; we all are one in call,

to plan and work to - geth-er that all may know Christ's love.
so ev - ery folk and na - tion may feel God's warm em - brace.
our var-ied gifts u - nit-ed by Christ, the Lord of all.

WORDS: Rusty Edwards (Matt. 28:19-20; 1 Cor. 12:4-6) KUORTANE
MUSIC: Finnish folk melody 76.76 D

2244   People Need the Lord

1. Peo-ple need the Lord,   peo-ple need the
2. Peo-ple need the Lord,   peo-ple need the

Lord;   at the end of bro - ken dreams,
Lord;   when will we re - al - ize

| 1 | 2 |

he's the o - pen door.   peo-ple need the Lord.

WORDS: Greg Nelson and Phill McHugh (John 4:35; 10:7)   PEOPLE NEED THE LORD
MUSIC: Greg Nelson and Phill McHugh   Irregular

© 1983 River Oaks Music Co., Inc./Shepherd's Fold Music

2245   Within the Day-to-Day
(A Hymn for Deacons)

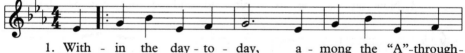

1. With - in the day - to - day,   a - mong the "A"-through-
(2. The) pal - ace has its place,   mu - se - ums play their
(3. The) sur - geon sews the heart,   the plumb - er tends the
(4. The) ex - ca - vat - ing God   un - earths new hope each

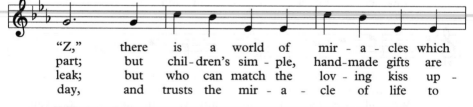

"Z,"   there is a world of mir - a - cles which
part;   but chil-dren's sim - ple, hand-made gifts are
leak;   but who can match the lov - ing kiss up -
day,   and trusts the mir - a - cle of life to

| 1 | 2 |

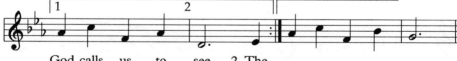

God calls us to see. 2. The
pre-cious, God - ly art. 3. The
on a tear-stained cheek? 4. The

us, the soul-filled clay.

WORDS: John Thornburg   TWENTY
MUSIC: Jane Marshall   SM

© 1999 Abingdon Press (admin. by The Copyright Co., Nashville, TN)

Word of God in Human Language 2246

1. Word of God in hu-man lan-guage for this time and in our tongue,
2. Ev-ery-where the world is hun-gry for the lib-er-a-ting Word,
3. So God's voice con-tin-ues speak-ing in the words we can't de-ny,

tell a-new the age-less sto-ry, ev-er an-cient, ev-er young.
food for spir-it as for bod-y, to be tast-ed, felt, and heard.
sound-ing out a-cross the ag-es. Will we an-swer or de-fy?

May our hearts re-ceive the mes-sage of God's faith-ful, lov-ing care;
It is thus the Word en-coun-ters at God's own ap-point-ed hour,
As the call be-comes still clear-er, wit-ness that the Word shall last,

may our lives re-spond in ac-tion, liv-ing deed and liv-ing prayer.
bring-ing knowl-edge and per-cep-tion of true jus-tice, peace, and power.
may we fol-low with com-mit-ment in the pres-ent as the past.

WORDS: Jane Parker Huber
MUSIC: John Zundel
Words © 1992 Jane Parker Huber

BEECHER
87.87 D

2247   Crashing Waters at Creation

1. Crash-ing wa-ters at cre-a-tion, or-dered by the
2. Part-ing wa-ter stood and trem-bled as the cap-tives
3. Cleans-ing wa-ter once at Jor-dan closed a-round the
4. Liv-ing wa-ter, nev-er en-ding, quench the thirst and

Spir-it's breath, first to wit-ness day's be-gin-ning
passed on through, wash-ing off the chains of bond-age—
one fore-told, o-pened to re-veal the glo-ry
flood the soul. Well-spring, Source of life e-ter-nal,

from the bright-ness of night's death. _____
chan-nel to a life made new. _____
ev-er new and ev-er old. _____
drench our dry-ness, make us whole. _____

WORDS: Sylvia G. Dunstan (Gen. 1:1-8; Exod. 14; Matt. 3; John 4:7-15)
MUSIC: William A. Cross

CRASHING WATERS
87.87

Creed One

2248

We be - lieve in God our Cre - a - tor and in

Je - sus Christ, God's on - ly Son, and in the Spir-it that

gives us the Word and the Love that makes us one. __

WORDS: Chip Andrus
MUSIC: Chip Andrus

CREED ONE
99.10 7

© 2000 Chip Andrus

God Claims You

2249

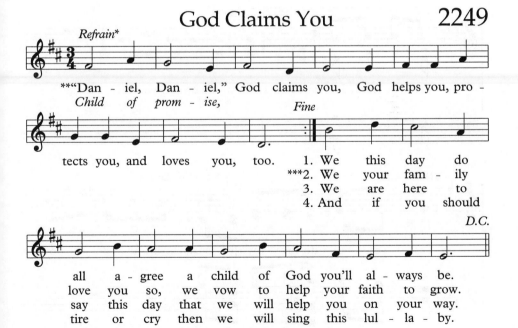

Refrain

**"Dan - iel, Dan - iel," God claims you, God helps you, pro -
Child of prom - ise,
Fine

tects you, and loves you, too.
1. We this day do
***2. We your fam - ily
3. We are here to
4. And if you should

D.C.

all	a - gree	a	child	of	God	you'll	al - ways	be.
love	you	so,	we	vow	to	help	your faith	to	grow.
say	this	day	that	we	will	help	you	on	your way.
tire	or	cry	then	we	will	sing	this	lul - la - by.

Sing Refrain twice at beginning and end, and once between stanzas.
**May insert child's name.*
***May insert parents' names "Jeff and Kathy love you so, we vow …"*

WORDS: Stanley M. Farr
MUSIC: Stanley M. Farr

FARR
Irregular with Refrain

© 1981 Stanley M. Farr

2250 I've Just Come from the Fountain

I've just come from the foun-tain, I've just come from the

foun-tain, Lord, I've just come from the foun-tain, his name's so

sweet. O Lord, I've sweet. 1. O broth-er, do you love Je-sus?

Yes,   yes,   I   do love my Je - sus. Broth-er, do you love

2. O sister, do you love Jesus ...   3. O sinner, do you love Jesus ...

WORDS: African American spiritual
MUSIC: African American spiritual; arr. by James Capers
Arr. © 1995 Augsburg Fortress from *With One Voice*

HIS NAME SO SWEET
88.74 with Refrain

Je - sus?　　His　name's　so　　sweet. O　Lord, I've

We Are Baptized in Christ Jesus　　2251

1. We are bap-tized in Christ Je-sus, we are bap-tized in　his　death.
2. In the wa-ter and the wit-ness, in the break-ing of　the　bread,
3. Glo-ry be to our cre-a-tor, glo-ry be　to Christ, the　Son;

For as Christ was raised vic - to-rious, we might live　a brand new　life.
in the wait-ing arms of　Je-sus, who is　ris-en from the　dead,
glo-ry to　the Ho-ly　Spir-it,　ev-er　three and ev-er　one.

And if　we have been u - nit-ed　in a　dread-ful death like　his,
we have found a　new be-gin-ning. In the ash-es of　our　past,
As it　was in　the be-gin-ning, glo-ry now re-sounds a - gain

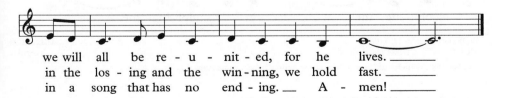

we will　all　be re-u - nit-ed, for　he　lives. _____
in the　los-ing and the　win-ning, we hold　fast. _____
in a　song that has　no　end-ing. __　A - men! _____

WORDS: John Ylvisaker (Rom. 6:3-5)　　　　　　　　　　　　　　OUIMETTE
MUSIC: John Ylvisaker　　　　　　　　　　　　　　　　　　　87.87.87.11

© 1985 John C. Ylvisaker

2252   Come, Be Baptized

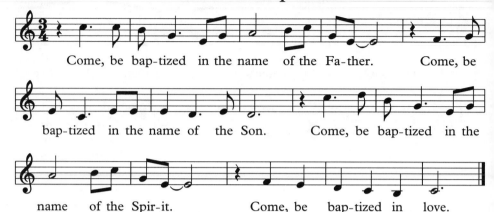

Come, be bap-tized in the name of the Fa-ther. Come, be bap-tized in the name of the Son. Come, be bap-tized in the name of the Spir-it. Come, be bap-tized in love.

Stanzas included in other editions.

WORDS: Gary Alan Smith (Matt. 28:19)   COME, BE BAPTIZED
MUSIC: Gary Alan Smith   Irregular

© 1982 Hope Publishing Co.

2253   Water, River, Spirit, Grace

Wa - ter, Riv - er, Spir - it, Grace, sweep o - ver me, sweep o - ver me! Re - carve the depths your fin-gers traced ____ in sculpt-ing me ____ in sculpt-ing me. ____

WORDS: Thomas H. Troeger   TRES RIOS
MUSIC: O. I. Cricket Harrison   Irregular

Words © 1987, 1991 Oxford University Press, Inc.; music © 1995 Chalice Press

BAPTISM, CONFIRMATION, REAFFIRMATION, *see further:*

2114   At the Font We Start Our Journey
2051   I Was There to Hear Your Borning Cry
2107   Wade in the Water

In Remembrance of Me

2254

1. In re - mem-brance of me, eat this bread. ___ In re -
(2. In re -) mem-brance of me, heal the sick. ___ In re -
(3. In re -) mem-brance of me, search for truth. ___ In re -

mem-brance of me, drink this wine. ___ In re-mem-brance of
mem-brance of me, feed the poor. ___ In re-mem-brance of
mem-brance of me, al - ways love. ___ In re-mem-brance of

Third time to Coda

me, pray for the time when God's own will is
me, o - pen the door and let your neigh - bors
me, don't look a - bove, but in your

1 **2**

done. ___ 2. In re - in, let them in. ___ Take,

eat, and be com - fort - ed; drink and re - mem - ber,

too, ___ that this is my bod - y and pre - cious

D.S. al Coda

blood shed for you, ___ shed for you. ___ 3. In re -

CODA

heart, ___ look for God. ___

Do this in re - mem-brance of me. ___

WORDS: Ragan Courtney (Matt. 6:10; 1 Cor. 11:23-25)
MUSIC: Buryl Red

RED
Irregular

© 1972 Broadman Press, assigned to Van Ness Press, Inc.

2255 In the Singing

1. In the sing-ing, in the si-lence, in the hands ex-pec-tant,
2. In the ques-tion, in the an-swer, in the mo-ment of ac -

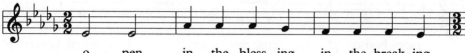

o - pen, in the bless - ing, in the break-ing,
cep - tance, in the heart's cry, in the heal - ing,

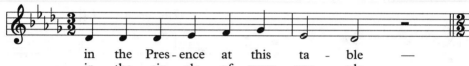

in the Pres - ence at this ta - ble —
in the cir - cle of your peo - ple —

Refrain

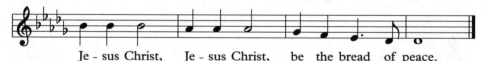

Je - sus Christ, Je - sus Christ, be the wine of grace:

Je - sus Christ, Je - sus Christ, be the bread of peace.

WORDS: Shirley Erena Murray
MUSIC: Carlton R. Young
© 1996 Hope Publishing Co.

BREAD OF PEACE
LM with Refrain

2256 Holy, Holy, Holy Lord
(Sanctus)

Part 1

1. Ho - ly, ho - ly, ho - ly Lord of
(2. Bless-ed,) bless-ed is he who comes in the

Part 2

1. Ho - ly, _____ ho - ly, ho - ly Lord of
(2. Bless-ed,) _ bless-ed is he who comes in the

WORDS: Trad. (Isa. 6:3; Matt. 21:9)
MUSIC: Iona Community (Scotland)
© WGRG The Iona Community (Scotland). Used by permission of GIA Publications, Inc.

SANCTUS (IONA)
Irregular

2257-a Communion Setting
(Preface)

WORDS: From *The United Methodist Hymnal*
MUSIC: Mark A. Miller

2257-b (Sanctus)

WORDS: From *The United Methodist Hymnal* (Isa. 6:3; Matt. 21:9)
MUSIC: Mark A. Miller

full　　　of　　　your　　　glo　　　　　　-

ry. ＿＿＿＿＿ Ho - san - na in the high - est! Ho -

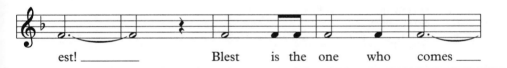

san - na in the high - est! Ho - san - na in the high　　　-

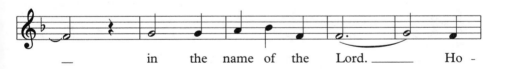

est! ＿＿＿＿ Blest　is the one　who　comes ＿＿

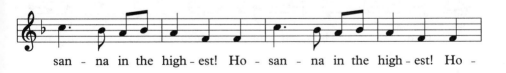

＿　　in　the name of the　Lord. ＿＿＿＿ Ho -

san - na in the high - est! Ho - san - na in the high - est! Ho -

san - na in the high　　-　　est! ＿＿＿＿＿

2257-c   (Memorial Acclamation)

Christ has died, Christ is ris - en,

Christ will come a - gain. _____ Ho -

san - na in the high - est! Ho - san - na in the high - est! Ho -

san - na in the high - est! _____

WORDS: From *The United Methodist Hymnal*
MUSIC: Mark A. Miller

Words © 1989 The United Methodist Publishing House (admin. by The Copyright Co., Nashville, TN); music © 1999 Abingdon
Press (admin. by The Copyright Co., Nashville, TN)

2257-d   (Great Amen)

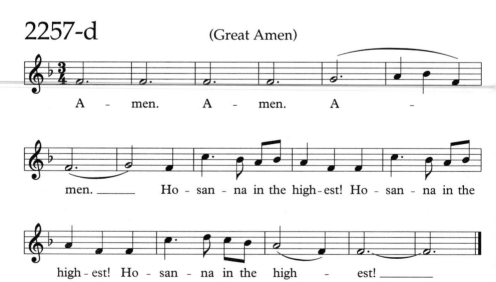

A - men. A - men. A -

men. _____ Ho - san - na in the high - est! Ho - san - na in the

high - est! Ho - san - na in the high - est! _____

WORDS: From *The United Methodist Hymnal*
MUSIC: Mark A. Miller

Words © 1989 The United Methodist Publishing House (admin. by The Copyright Co., Nashville, TN); music © 1999 Abingdon
Press (admin. by The Copyright Co., Nashville, TN)

Sing Alleluia to the Lord

2258

Descant

(Lord!)   1. Sing   al – le – lu – ia   to the

Melody

1. Sing   al – le – lu – ia   to the   Lord!

Lord!   (All stanzas) Sing   al – le – lu – ia,

Sing   al – le – lu – ia   to the   Lord!

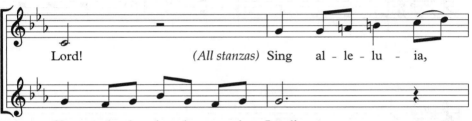

al   –   le   –   lu   –   ia!

Sing   al – le – lu – ia,   sing   al – le – lu – ia!

Final ending

(1.) Sing   al – le – lu – ia   to the   Lord!

Sing   al – le – lu – ia   to the   Lord!

2. Lift up your hearts unto the Lord …
3. In Christ the world has been redeemed …
4. His resurrection sets us free …
5. Therefore we celebrate the feast …
6. Sing alleluia to the Lord …

WORDS: Sts. 1, 6 by Linda Stassen; sts. 2-5 from early Christian liturgy (1 Cor. 5:8)
MUSIC: Linda Stassen

SING ALLELUIA
Irregular

2259　　　　　Victim Divine

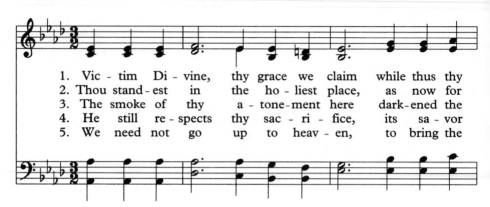

1. Vic - tim Di - vine, thy grace we claim while thus thy
2. Thou stand - est in the ho - liest place, as now for
3. The smoke of thy a - tone-ment here dark-ened the
4. He still re - spects thy sac - ri - fice, its sa - vor
5. We need not go up to heav - en, to bring the

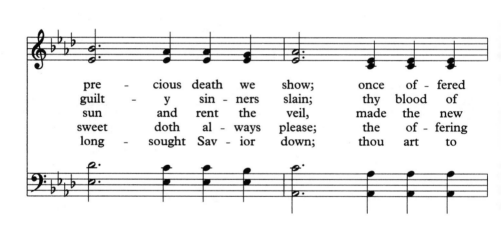

pre - cious death we show; once of - fered
guilt - y sin - ners slain; thy blood of
sun and rent the veil, made the new
sweet doth al - ways please; the of - fering
long - sought Sav - ior down; thou art to

up, a spot - less Lamb, in thy great
sprink - ling speaks, and prays, all - prev - a -
way to heaven ap - pear, and showed the
smokes through earth and skies, dif - fus - ing
all al - read - y given, thou dost e'en

WORDS: Charles Wesley (Heb. 10:12-22)　　　　　　　　　　　SELENA
MUSIC: Isaac B. Woodbury　　　　　　　　　　　　　　　　88.88.88

tem - ple here be - low, thou didst for all our kind a -
lent for help - less ones; thy blood is still our ran - som
great In - vis - i - ble; well pleased in thee our God looked
life, and joy, and peace; to these thy low - er courts it
now thy ban - quet crown: To ev - ery faith - ful soul ap -

tone, and stand - est now be - fore the throne.
found, and spreads sal - va - tion all a - round.
down, and called his reb - els to a crown.
comes, and fills them with di - vine per - fumes.
pear, and show thy real pres - ence here!

Let Us Be Bread   2260

Let us be bread, blessed by the Lord, bro - ken and

shared, life for the world. Let us be wine,

love free - ly poured. Let us be one in the Lord. _____

Stanzas included in other editions.

WORDS: Thomas Porter

MUSIC: Thomas Porter

LET US BE BREAD
Irregular

© 1990 GIA Publications, Inc.

2261   Life-giving Bread

Life - giv - ing bread, _____ as our hearts are trans -

formed a - new, _____ and life - giv - ing wine, ___

___ may we share in a life with you. _____

Stanzas included in other editions.

WORDS: Ricky Manalo (John 6:35, 48)   MANALO
MUSIC: Ricky Manalo   Irregular

2262   Let Us Offer to the Father
(Te Ofrecemos Padre Nuestro)

Refrain

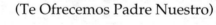
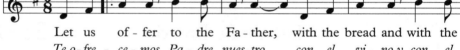
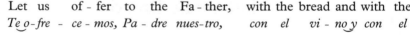

Let us of - fer to the Fa - ther, with the bread and with the
Te o-fre - ce - mos, Pa - dre nues-tro, con el vi - no y con el

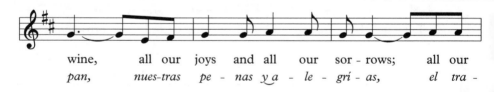

wine, all our joys and all our sor - rows; all our
pan, nues-tras pe - nas y a - le - grí - as, el tra -

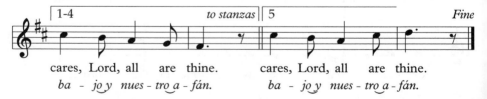

|1-4| to stanzas |5| | Fine|

cares, Lord, all are thine.   cares, Lord, all are thine.
ba - jo y nues - tro a - fán.   ba - jo y nues - tro a - fán.

WORDS: From the *Misa Popular Nicaragüense;* trans. by Alice Parker   OFERTORIO
MUSIC: From the *Misa Popular Nicaragüense;* arr. by Raquel Mora Martínez   87.87 with Refrain

1. As the grow - ing wheat will ri - pen let us
2. Let the poor and heav - y la - den gath - er
1. Co - mo el tri - go de los cam - pos en un
2. A los po - bres de la tie - rra, a los

show to all the world we can grow and ri - pen
at the Sav - ior's sign, where their grief will turn to
pan se con - vir - tió, a - sí haz de nues - tras
que su - frien - do es - tán, cam - bia su do - lor en

(Refrain)

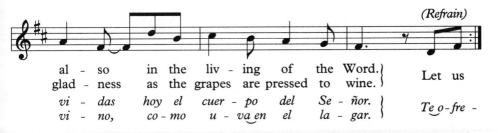

al - so in the liv - ing of the Word.⎰
glad - ness as the grapes are pressed to wine.⎱   Let us

vi - das hoy el cuer - po del Se - ñor.⎰
vi - no, co - mo u - va en el la - gar.⎱   Te o - fre -

3. From the country, from the city,
   from the riches of the land,
   we bring back to our Creator
   many gifts of heart and hand.

4. All your people here together
   bring you offerings of love,
   joining with your whole creation,
   seeking liberty and peace.

5. Glory be to God, the Father
   and to Christ, the living Son,
   who together with the Spirit
   make the holy Three-in-One.

3. *Estos dones son el signo*
   del esfuerzo de unidad
   que la humanidad realiza
   en el campo y la ciudad.

4. *Es tu pueblo quien te ofrece,*
   con los dones del altar,
   la naturaleza entera,
   anhelando libertad.

5. *Gloria sea dada al Padre*
   y a su Hijo Redentor
   y al Espíritu Divino
   que nos llena de su amor.

2263 **Broken for Me**

1. He of-fered his bod - y; ___ he poured out his soul;
2. ___ Come to my ta - ble ___ ___ and with me dine;
3. ___ This is my bod - y ___ ___ giv - en for you;
4. ___ This is my blood ___ ___ I shed for you,

Je - sus was bro - ken ___ that we might be whole.
eat of my bread ___ and drink of my wine.
eat it, re-mem - bering ___ ___ I died for you.
for your for-give - ness, ___ ___ mak-ing you new.

WORDS: Janet Lunt (1 Cor. 11:23-25)
MUSIC: Janet Lunt

© 1978 Sovereign Music UK

BROKEN FOR ME
Irregular with Refrain

2264 **Come to the Table**

Come to the ta-ble of mer - cy, pre-pared with the wine and the

bread. All who are hun-gry and thirst - y,

WORDS: Claire Cloninger
MUSIC: Martin J. Nystrom

© 1991 Word Music, Inc. and Integrity's Hosanna! Music and Juniper Landing Music

TABLE OF MERCY
Irregular

come and your souls will be fed. Come at the Lord's in - vi -

ta - tion; re - ceive from his nail - scarred hand.

Eat of the bread of sal - va - tion; drink of the blood of the Lamb.

Time Now to Gather   2265

1. Time now to gath - er, time now to feel
2. Time to re - mem - ber Christ who was sent.
3. All who are hun - gry, come, and be fed.

Christ's ho - ly pres - ence grac - ing this meal.
Time to say, "Thank you" for all he meant.
Serve one an - oth - er this cup and bread.

Grain from the har - vest, fruit of the vine;
Come to this ta - ble. Come, with - out fear.
All who are trou - bled, hurt - ing, or sad,

sim - ple the sup - per, sa - cred the sign.
God will for - give you, wel - come you here.
come, and find heal - ing. Come, and be glad!

WORDS: Mary Nelson Keithahn (Luke 22:19-20)
MUSIC: John D. Horman

WELCOME SONG
54.54 D

2266   Here Is Bread, Here Is Wine

1. Here is bread,   here is wine:
2. Here is grace,   here is peace:
3. Here we are,   joined in one:

Christ is with us:

He is with us.

Break the bread;   taste the wine:
Know his grace;   find his peace:
We'll pro-claim   till he comes

| 1 | 2, 3 | *Refrain* |

Christ is with us   here.
Feast on Je - sus   here.   In this bread
Je - sus cru - ci -   fied.

there is heal - ing;   in this cup there's life for - ev - er.

In this mo - ment   by the Spir - it   Christ is with us here.

WORDS: Graham Kendrick
MUSIC: Graham Kendrick

HERE IS BREAD
68.65 with Refrain

© 1991 Make Way Music (admin. by Music Services in the Western Hemisphere)

2267   Taste and See

Taste and see,   taste and see   the good - ness

of the Lord. _____   O taste and see,   taste and

Stanzas included in other editions.

WORDS: James E. Moore (Ps. 34:8)
MUSIC: James E. Moore

TASTE AND SEE
Irregular with Refrain

© 1983 GIA Publications, Inc.

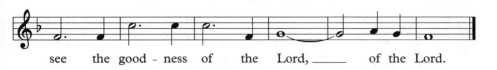

see the good - ness of the Lord, _____ of the Lord.

As We Gather at Your Table   2268

1. As we gath - er at your ta - ble, as we
2. Turn our wor - ship in - to wit - ness in the
3. Gra - cious Spir - it, help us sum - mon oth - er

lis - ten to your word, help us know, O God, your
sac - ra-ment of life; send us forth to love and
guests to share that feast where tri - um - phant Love will

pres - ence; let our hearts and minds be
serve you, bring - ing peace where there is
wel - come those who had been last and

stirred. Nour-ish us with sa - cred sto - ry till we
strife. Give us, Christ, your great com - pas - sion to for -
least. There no more will en - vy blind us nor will

claim it as our own; teach us through this ho - ly
give as you for - gave; may we still be - hold your
pride our peace de - stroy, as we join with saints and

ban - quet how to make Love's vic - tory known.
im - age in the world you died to save.
an - gels to re - peat the sound - ing joy.

WORDS: Carl P. Daw Jr.   RAQUEL
MUSIC: Skinner Chávez-Melo   87.87 D

Words © 1989 Hope Publishing Co.; music © 1985 Skinner Chávez-Melo

2269 # Come, Share the Lord

1. We gath-er here in Je-sus' name, his love is
(3. He joins us) here, he breaks the bread, the Lord who
(5. We'll gath-er) soon where an-gels sing; we'll see the

burn-ing in our hearts like liv-ing flame; for through the
pours the cup is ris-en from the dead; the one we
glo-ry of our Lord and com-ing King; now we an-

lov-ing Son the Fa-ther makes us one:)
love the most is now our gra-cious host: } Come, take the
ti-ci-pate the feast for which we wait:)

Fine

bread; come, drink the wine; come, share the Lord.

2. No one is a stran-ger here, ___ ev-ery-one be-
4. We are now a fam-i-ly of which the Lord is

longs; find-ing our for-give-ness here, we in
head; though un-seen he meets us here in the

turn for-give all wrongs.   3. He joins us
break-ing of the bread.   5. We'll gath-er

WORDS: Bryan Jeffery Leech   DIVERNON
MUSIC: Bryan Jeffery Leech   Irregular
© 1984, 1987 Fred Bock Music Co.

EUCHARIST (HOLY COMMUNION, LORD'S SUPPER), *see further:*

2126   All Who Hunger

He Has Made Me Glad

2270

I will en-ter his gates with thanks-giv-ing in my heart, I will

en - ter his courts with praise. I will

say, "This is the day that the Lord has made." I

will re - joice, for he has made me glad.

Refrain

He has made me glad, he has made me glad. I

will re - joice, for he has made me glad.

He has made me glad, he has made me glad. I

will re - joice, for he has made me glad.

WORDS: Leona Von Brethorst (Ps. 100:2, 4; 118:24)   LEONA
MUSIC: Leona Von Brethorst   Irregular with Refrain

© 1976 Maranatha Praise, Inc. (admin. by The Copyright Co., Nashville, TN)

2271 Come! Come! Everybody Worship
(Vengan Todos Adoremos)

Refrain

Come! Come! Ev-ery-bod-y wor-ship with a prayer or song of praise!
¡Ven - gan to-dos a-do-re-mos con can-tos y o-ra-ción!

Fine

Come! Come! Ev-ery-bod-y wor-ship! Wor-ship God al-ways!
¡Ven - gan to-dos a-do-re-mos a nues-tro Se - ñor!

1. Wor-ship and re-mem-ber to keep the Sab-bath day.
2. Wor-ship and re-mem-ber the Lord's un-end-ing care,
3. Wor-ship and re-mem-ber your bless-ings great and small.
4. Wor-ship and re-mem-ber how Je-sus long a-go
5. Wor-ship and re-mem-ber that God is like a light,

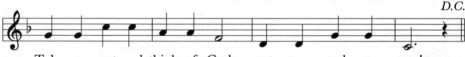

D.C.

Take a rest and think of God; put your work a-way!
reach-ing out to love and help peo-ple ev-ery-where!
Give to God an of-fer-ing; show your thanks for all!
taught us how to talk to God; some-thing we should know!
show-ing you the way to go; ev-er burn-ing bright!

WORDS: Natalie Sleeth; Spanish trans. by Maria Luiza Santillán de Baert
MUSIC: Natalie Sleeth

NATALIE
66.75 with Refrain

2272 Holy Ground

We are stand-ing ___ on ho-ly ground, ___

___ and I know that there are an-gels all a-

WORDS: Geron Davis (Exod. 3:5)
MUSIC: Geron Davis

HOLY GROUND
Irregular

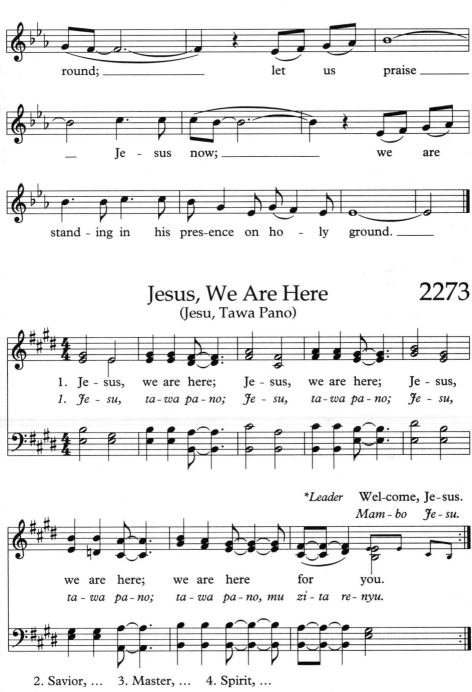

round; _____ let us praise _____

_ Je - sus now; _____ we are

stand - ing in his pres-ence on ho - ly ground. _____

Jesus, We Are Here   2273
(Jesu, Tawa Pano)

1. Je - sus, we are here; Je - sus, we are here; Je - sus,
1. *Je - su, ta - wa pa - no; Je - su, ta - wa pa - no; Je - su,*

Leader Wel-come, Je-sus.
Mam - bo   Je - su.

we are here; we are here for you.
ta - wa pa - no; ta - wa pa - no, mu zi - ta re - nyu.

2. Savior, ...   3. Master, ...   4. Spirit, ...

Omit last time.

WORDS: Patrick Matsikenyiri
MUSIC: Patrick Matsikenyiri

MATSIKENYIRI
Irregular

© 1990, 1996 General Board of Global Ministries, GBGMusik

2274

Come, All You People
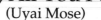
(Uyai Mose)

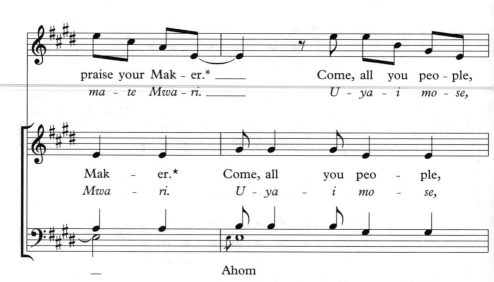

Other words may be substituted such as "Savior," "Spirit," and so forth.

WORDS: Alexander Gondo
MUSIC: Alexander Gondo; arr. by John Bell

UYAI MOSE
Irregular

2275

Kyrie

Ky - ri - e, Ky - ri - e e - le - i -

son. Ky - ri - e, Ky - ri - e

e - le - i - son. Chri - ste, Chri - ste

e - le - i - son. Chri - ste, Chri - ste

e - le - i - son. Ky - ri - e, Ky - ri - e

e - le - i - son. Ky - ri - e, Ky - ri - e

e - le - i - son, e - le - i - son.

WORDS: Ancient Greek
MUSIC: Based on Mvt. II from *Symphony No. 9* by Antonín Dvořák;
       arr. by Ruth Elaine Schram

NEW WORLD
Irregular

Glory to God in the Highest 2276

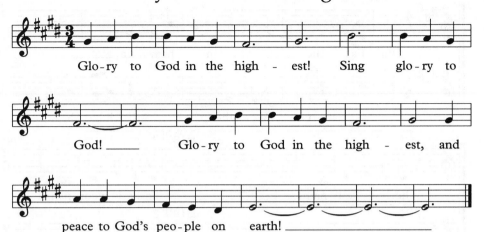

Glo-ry to God in the high - est! Sing glo-ry to

God! ____ Glo-ry to God in the high - est, and

peace to God's peo-ple on earth! _____

Stanzas included in other editions.

WORDS: From the liturgy (Luke 2:14)
MUSIC: David Haas from *Mass of Light*

© 1988 GIA Publications, Inc.

GLORIA (HAAS)
Irregular

Lord, Have Mercy 2277

Lord, have mer - cy. Christ, have mer - cy.

Fine

Lord, have mer - cy on us. _____

Though red like crim-son is my sin, _____ great - er

D.C. al Fine

yet is for - give - ness found in Christ. _____

WORDS: Swee Hong Lim (Isa. 1:18)
MUSIC: Swee Hong Lim

© 1995 General Board of Global Ministries, GBGMusik

SINGAPURA
Irregular

The Lord's Prayer

2278

WORDS: Jim Strathdee (Matt. 6:9-13)
MUSIC: Anon.; arr. by Al Oppenheimer
© 1977 Desert Flower Music

LORD'S PRAYER (OPPENHEIMER)
Irregular

2279   The Trees of the Field

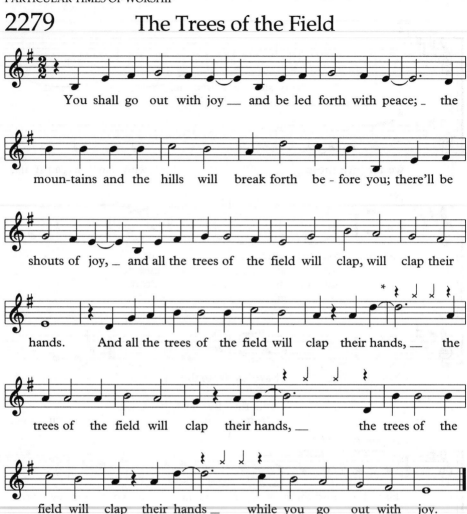

You shall go out with joy __ and be led forth with peace; _ the
moun-tains and the hills will break forth be - fore you; there'll be
shouts of joy, _ and all the trees of the field will clap, will clap their
hands. And all the trees of the field will clap their hands, __ the
trees of the field will clap their hands, __ the trees of the
field will clap their hands _ while you go out with joy.

*Clap hands.

WORDS: Steffi Geiser Ruben (Isa. 55:12)
MUSIC: Stuart Dauermann

THE TREES OF THE FIELD
Irregular

© 1975 Lillenas Publishing Co. (admin. by The Copyright Co., Nashville, TN)

2280   The Lord Bless and Keep You

The Lord bless and keep you, the Lord make his
(The) Lord bless and keep you, the Lord lift his

WORDS: Jim Strathdee (Num. 6:24-26)
MUSIC: Jim Strathdee

STRATHDEE BENEDICTION
Irregular

© 1981 Desert Flower Music

face   to   shine   on   you and be   gra - cious,   gra
coun - te - nance on   you and give   peace, _____   give   you

cious. The

peace. Sha - lom. _____   Sha - lom. _____
(__   A   -   men.) _____

May You Run and Not Be Weary   2281

May you   run   and not   be   wea - ry.   May your

heart   be   filled   with   song. __   And may the

love of God   con - tin - ue   to give you hope   and

keep you   strong. And may you   run   and not   be   wea -

ry.   May your life be filled with joy! __   And may the

road   you trav - el   al-ways   lead   you   home. _

WORDS: Handt Hanson and Paul Murakami (Isa. 40:31)   PRINCE OF PEACE
MUSIC: Handt Hanson and Paul Murakami   Irregular

© 1991 Changing Church Forum

2282

I'll Fly Away

WORDS: Albert E. Brumley (Isa. 55:6; 2 Cor. 5:8)
MUSIC: Albert E. Brumley

I'LL FLY AWAY
94.94 with Refrain

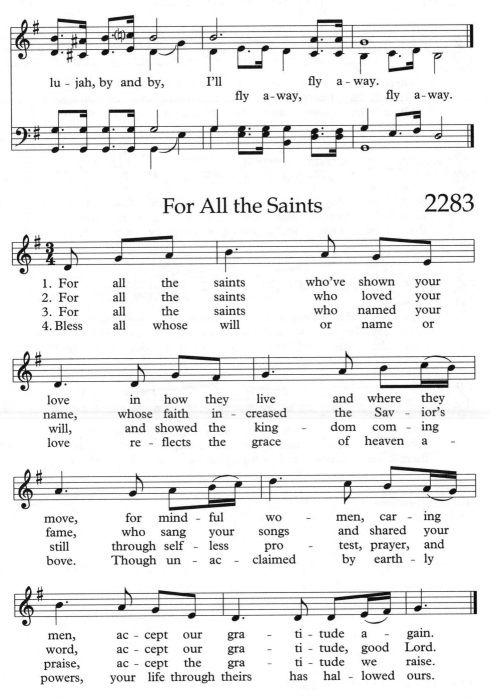

lu - jah, by and by, I'll fly a - way.
fly a - way, fly a - way.

For All the Saints 2283

1. For all the saints who've shown your
2. For all the saints who loved your
3. For all the saints who named your
4. Bless all whose will or name or

love in how they live and where they
name, whose faith in - creased the Sav - ior's
will, and showed the king - dom com - ing
love re - flects the grace of heaven a -

move, for mind - ful wo - men, car - ing
fame, who sang your songs and shared your
still through self - less pro - test, prayer, and
bove. Though un - ac - claimed by earth - ly

men, ac - cept our gra - ti - tude a - gain.
word, ac - cept our gra - ti - tude, good Lord.
praise, ac - cept the gra - ti - tude we raise.
powers, your life through theirs has hal - lowed ours.

WORDS: John Bell
MUSIC: English folk melody

O WALY WALY
LM

Words © 1996 WGRG The Iona Community (Scotland). Used by permission of GIA Publications, Inc.

2284 Joy in the Morning

1. There'll be joy in the morn-ing on that day,
2. There'll be peace and con-tent-ment ev - er - more,
3. There'll be love and for - give-ness ev - ery - where,

there'll be joy in the morn-ing on that day,
there'll be peace and con-tent-ment ev - er - more,
there'll be love and for - give-ness ev - ery - where,

for the day - light will dawn when the dark - ness is gone,
ev - ery heart, ev - ery voice on that day will re - joice,
and the way of the Lord will that day be re-stored,

there'll be joy in the morn-ing on that day.
there'll be peace and con-tent-ment ev - er - more.
there'll be love and for - give-ness ev - ery - where.

WORDS: Natalie Sleeth (Ps. 30:5)
MUSIC: Natalie Sleeth

JOY IN THE MORNING
Irregular

© 1977 Hope Publishing Co.

ACKNOWLEDGMENTS

Use of copyrighted material is gratefully acknowledged by the publisher. Every effort has been made to locate the administrator of each copyright. The publisher would be pleased to have any errors or omissions brought to its attention. All copyright notices include the following declarations: All rights reserved. International copyright secured. Used with permission.

Abingdon Press (see The Copyright Company)

Above the Rim Music (ASCAP) (see BMG Songs, Inc.)

Doris Akers (see Hal Leonard Corporation)

Albert E. Brumley & Sons (SESAC) (see Integrated Copyright Group)

Alfred Publishing Co., Inc.; 16320 Roscoe Blvd.; Van Nuys, CA 91406; FAX (818) 891-5999

Chip Andrus; c/o Presbyterian Church (USA); 100 Witherspoon St., Louisville, KY 40202; (502) 569-5000

Ariose Music (ASCAP) (see EMI Christian Music Group)

Augsburg Fortress Publishers; P.O. Box 1209; Minneapolis, MN 55440-1209; (612) 330-3300

Belwin-Mills Publishing Corp. (see Warner Bros. Publications)

Birdwing Music (ASCAP) (see EMI Christian Music Group)

BMG Songs (ASCAP) (see EMI Christian Music Group)

BMG Songs, Inc. (ASCAP); 741 Cool Springs Blvd.; Franklin, TN 37067; (615) 261-3300

Brentwood-Benson Music Publishing, Inc. (ASCAP); Attn: Copyright Administration; 741 Cool Springs Blvd.; Franklin, TN 37067

Brier Patch Music; 4324 Canal Southwest; Grandville, MI 49418

Broadman Press (see Van Ness Press, Inc.)

Bud John Songs, Inc. (ASCAP) (see EMI Christian Music Group)

Carol Joy Music (ASCAP) (see Integrated Copyright Group)

Chalice Press; Christian Board of Publication; 1221 Locust St., Suite 1200; St. Louis, MO 63103; FAX (314) 231-2027

Changing Church Forum; 13901 Fairview Drive; Burnsville, MN 55337; (800) 874-2044; FAX (952) 435-8015

Skinner Chávez-Melo; c/o Juan Francisco Chávez-Melo; Juarez no. 85 Casa 19; Col. Ampliacion Miguel Hidalgo; Tlalpan 14250; Mexico D. F. Mexico; (011) 525-528-1884; chavezme@prodigy.net.mx

Susan Palo Cherwien (see Augsburg Fortress Publishers)

Choristers Guild; 2834 W. Kingsley Rd.; Garland, TX 75041-2498; (972) 271-1521; FAX (972) 840-3113; www.choristersguild.org

J. Jefferson Cleveland (see William B. McClain)

Cokesbury (see The Copyright Company)

Common Cup Co.; 7591 Gray Ave.; Burnby BC V5J 3ZY; (604) 434-8323

Concordia Publishing House; 3558 South Jefferson Ave; St. Louis, MO 63118-3968; (314) 268-1000; www.cph.org

William A. Cross, 80 Plaza Drive, Apt. 2201, Winnipeg MB R3T 5S2, Canada

Damean Music (see GIA Publications, Inc.)

Dayspring Music, Inc. (see Word Music Group, Inc.)

Desert Flower Music; P.O. Box 1476; Carmichael, CA 95609

Andrew Donaldson; 14 Hambly Ave.; Toronto, Ontario M4E 2R6; FAX (416) 690-9967

Doubleday; 1745 Broadway; New York, NY 10019; (212) 782-8957; FAX (212) 782-8898

Dr. Margaret P. Douroux; Rev. Earl Pleasant Publishing; P.O. Box 3247; Thousand Oaks, CA 91359; FAX (818) 991-2567; GospelMeg@aol.com

Delores Dufner (see OCP Publications)

Sylvia G. Dunstan (see GIA Publications, Inc.)

Earthsongs; 220 NW 29th St.; Corallis, OR 97330; FAX (541) 754-5887

EMI Christian Music Group; P.O. Box 5085; 101 Winners Circle; Brentwood, TN 37024-5085; (615) 371-4300; FAX (615) 371-6897

Stanley M. Farr; 518 Fairmont Rd.; Morgantown, WV 26501

F.E.L. Publications (see The Lorenz Corporation)

Arthur Frackenpohl, 13 Hillcrest Dr., Potsdam, NY 13676.

Fred Bock Music Co., Inc.; P.O. Box 570567; Tarzana, CA 91357; (818) 996-6181; FAX (818) 996-2043; www.fredbockmusiccompany.com

Gamut Music Productions; 704 Saddle Trail Ct.; Hermitage, TN 37076

General Board of Global Ministries, GBGMusik; 475 Riverside Dr.; Room 350; New York, NY 10115

GIA Publications, Inc.; 7404 S. Mason Ave.; Chicago, IL 60638; (800) GIA-1358; FAX (708) 496-3828

Carolyn Winfrey Gillette; First Presbyterian Church; 305 South Broadway; Pitman, NJ 08071; FAX (856) 589-1051

Hal Leonard Corp.; 7777 W. Bluemound Rd.; Milwaukee, WI 53213; FAX (414) 774-3259

Marilyn Houser Hamm; Box 1887; Altona, Manitoba; Canada R0G 0B0; FAX (204) 831-5675; rhamm@mts.net

Harold Flammer, Inc. a division of Shawnee Press, Inc.; c/o Music Sales Corp.; www.musicsales.com

Harper Collins Religious (see The Copyright Company)

Carl Haywood; 5228 Foxboro Landing; Virginia Beach, VA 23464; FAX (757) 467-2172

Hinshaw Music, Inc.; P.O. Box 470; Chapel Hill, NC 27514-0470; FAX (919) 967-3399

Hodder and Stoughton Limited; 338 Euston Rd.; London, NW1 3BH, England; FAX 020-787-36308

Hope Publishing Company; 380 S. Main Pl.; Carol Stream, IL 60188; (800) 323-1049; FAX (630) 665-2552; www.hopepublishing.com

Jane Parker Huber (see Westminster John Knox Press)

Coni Huisman; 3239 Pettis Ave., NE; Ada, MI 49301

Integrated Copyright Group; P.O. Box 24149; Nashville, TN 37202

Integrity Music, Inc.; 1000 Cody Rd.; Mobile, AL 36695; (251) 633-9000; FAX (251) 776-5036

Integrity's Hosanna! Music (ASCAP); c/o Integrity Music, Inc.; 1000 Cody Rd.; Mobile, AL 36695-3425; (251) 633-9000; FAX (251) 776-5036

John T. Benson Publishing Co. (ASCAP) (see Brentwood-Benson Music Publishing, Inc.)

Jonathan Mark Music (ASCAP) (see EMI Christian Music Group)

Jubilate Hymns (see Hope Publishing Company)

Ron Klusmeier; 345 Pym St.; Parksville, B.C., Canada V9P 1C8; FAX (250) 954-1683; www.musiklus.com

Latter Rain Music (ASCAP) (see EMI Christian Music Group)

Geonyong Lee; KNUA; 1753 Seocho-dong; Seocho-gu; Seoul, Korea 137-070

Les Presses de Taizé (see GIA Publications, Inc.)

Lillenas Publishing Company (see The Copyright Company)

Lutheran Book of Worship (see Augsburg Fortress Publishers)

William B. McClain; c/o The Estate of J. Jefferson Cleveland; 4500 Massachusetts Ave., NW; Washington, D.C. 20016; FAX (301) 567-9776

Make Way Music (see Music Services, Inc.)

Maranatha! Music (see The Copyright Company)

ACKNOWLEDGMENTS

Maranatha Praise, Inc. (see The Copyright Company)

Martin and Morris (see Hal Leonard Corporation)

Matters Most Music (ASCAP) (see Brentwood-Benson Music Publishing, Inc.)

Meadowgreen Music Company (ASCAP) (see EMI Christian Music Group)

Mercy/Vineyard Publishing (see Music Services, Inc.)

Mole End Music (see Brentwood-Benson Music Publishing, Inc.)

Mountain Spring Music (ASCAP) (see EMI Christian Music Group)

Music Services, Inc. (ASCAP); 209 Chapelwood Dr.; Franklin, TN 37069; (615) 794-9015; FAX (615) 794-0793; www.musicservices.org

New Song Creations; 175 Heggie Lane; Erin, TN 37061

New Spring Publishing, Inc. (ASCAP) (see Brentwood-Benson Music Publishing, Inc.)

OCP Publications; Attn: Licensing Dept.; 5536 NE Hassalo; Portland, OR 97213; (800) 548-8749; FAX (503) 282-3486; liturgy@ocp.org

Oxford University Press, Inc.; 198 Madison Ave.; New York, NY 10016-4314; (212) 726-6000; FAX (212) 726-6441

Pilot Point Music (see The Copyright Company)

Prism Tree Music (see The Lorenz Corporation)

John S. Rice; Estate of John S. Rice; c/o Brian H. Davidson, Executor; 819 Sunnydale Rd.; Knoxville, TN 37923

River Oaks Music Company (BMI) (see EMI Christian Music Group)

Julian B. Rush; 1433 Williams St.; Unit 302; Denver, CO 80218-2531

Scripture in Song (ASCAP) (see Integrity Music, Inc.)

Selah Publishing Co. Inc.; 58 Pearl St.; Kingston, NY 12401; (845) 338-2816; FAX (845) 338-2991; (www.selahpub.com)

Shepherd's Fold Music (BMI) (see EMI Christian Music Group)

Singspiration Music (ASCAP) (see Brentwood-Benson Music Publishing, Inc.)

Songchannel Music Co. (ASCAP) (see EMI Christian Music Group)

SongWard Music (see Brentwood-Benson Music Publishing, Inc.)

Pablo Sosa, Eparlaco 634; 1406 Buenos Aires, Argentina

Sound III, Inc. (see Universal-MCA Music Publishing)

Sovereign Music UK; P.O. Box 356; Leighton Buzzard; LU7 3WP UK; 44-1-525-385578; FAX 44-1-525-372743; Sovereignmusic@aol.com

Linda Stassen (see New Song Creations)

Straightway Music (ASCAP) (see EMI Christian Music Group)

Thank You Music (see EMI Christian Music Group)

The Copyright Company; 1025 16th Avenue, South; Suite 204; Nashville, TN 37212; FAX (615) 321-1099

The Kruger Organization, Inc.; 15 Rolling Way; New York, NY 10956-6912; (202) 966-3280; FAX (202) 364-1367

The Lorenz Corporation; 501 East Third St.; Dayton, OH 45402; (937) 228-6118; FAX (937) 223-2042

The Pilgrim Press; 700 Prospect Ave., E.; Cleveland, OH 44115; pilgrimpress.com

The United Methodist Publishing House (see The Copyright Company)

John Thornburg; 9553 Atherton Drive; Dallas, TX 75243

Desmond Tutu (see Doubleday and Hodder & Stoughton)

Unichappell Music, Inc. (see Hal Leonard Corporation)

Universal-MCA Music Publishing (see Warner Bros. Publications U.S., Inc.)

Universal-PolyGram International Publishing, Inc. (see Warner Bros. Publications U.S., Inc.)

Utryck (see Walton Music Corporation)

Utterbach Music, Inc. (see Warner Bros. Publications U.S., Inc.)

Van Ness Press, Inc.; One Lifeway Plaza; Nashville, TN 37234-0187

Christopher Walker (see OCP Publications)

Mary Lu Walker; 16 Brown Rd.; Corning, NY 14830

Walton Music Corporation; P.O. Box 167; Bynum, NC 27228; FAX (919) 542-5527; www.waltonmusic.com

Warner Bros. Publications U.S., Inc.; 15800 Northwest 48th Ave.; Miami, FL 33014; (305) 521-1600; FAX (305) 625-3480

John Weaver; c/o Madison Avenue Presbyterian Church; 921 Madison Avenue; NY, NY 10021

Westminster John Knox Press; 100 Witherspoon St.; Louisville, KY 40202-1396; (502) 569-5060; FAX (502) 569-5113

WGRG; The Iona Community (Scotland) (See GIA Publications, Inc.)

Whole Armor/Full Armor Music (see The Kruger Organization, Inc.)

Word Music, Inc. (see Word Music Group, Inc.)

Word Music Group, Inc.; 20 Music Square East, Nashville, TN 37203

John Ylvisaker; Box 321; Waverly, IA 50677

Zimbel Press; 1595 Plank Road; Webster, NY 14580-9327

Darlene Zschech (ASCAP) (see Integrity's Hosanna! Music)

INDEX OF FIRST LINES AND COMMON TITLES

INDEX OF FIRST LINES AND COMMON TITLES

INDEX OF FIRST LINES AND COMMON TITLES